4 KEYS TO COLLEGE ADMISSIONS SUCCESS

Praise for
4 KEYS TO COLLEGE ADMISSIONS SUCCESS

From parents:

Imagine my son's delight when he received 11 acceptance letters. His mom and I are so proud. Thanks to Pamela Donnelly and her fine staff for all their support. Now the power is in our hands to decide where he will attend, instead of the other way around. What a feeling!

—Phil Reeves
Professional Actor (*Veep, Parks and Recreation*)/Dad

Our daughter not only got into the right college, but she was prepared for a successful transition from high school courses to college-level work as a result of working with these strategies. She is now thriving in her second year. Pamela Donnelly uniquely positioned her, and we love that she can still connect from her school on the East Coast via Skype with Pamela and her staff. Thank you!

—Chuck Pratt, Jr., Emmy Award–Winning
Television Writer (*General Hospital, All My Children*)/Dad

As the father of the teen actor who played Superman in the motion picture *Man of Steel*, my wife and I are grateful to Pamela Donnelly. Because of the scores our son Dylan achieved working with her staff on an important exam, he went from that breakthrough role in a major film to booking a terrific recurring role in the television series *Teen Wolf*. Pamela's support, strategic direction and quality tutors successfully guided us through the necessary process to help our son accomplish his academic objectives. We look forward to continuing to rely upon her guidance for the road ahead.

—**Carl Sprayberry**, Hotel General Manager/Dad

My daughter had a wonderful time taking Pamela Donnelly's Ivy League Writing Immersion class during the summer of her junior year, and it's her writing ability that really ended up making the greatest impact on her college admissions results. Djaq received a card signed by the entire admissions office at her #1 choice, Knox College, and was told that the Writers' Scholarship she won is the highest amount they've ever awarded.

She plans to double major there in creative writing and pre-med. Thank you, Pamela, for your guidance, and for being our cheerleader throughout the process.

—**Cathy Flynn**, Television Sound Editor/Mom

My daughter is on her way to her dream school, American University, with $40,000 in scholarships as a result of working with Pamela Donnelly and her colleagues. We counted on her every step of the way during the college applications process and got a great result.

—**Julie Napoleon**, High School Teacher/Mom

Working with an expert who is also a mother was great. I looked at many other options before deciding whom to work with, and chose Pamela Donnelly. I know she and her staff do what they do because they actually care about students, and that is important to me as a parent. Others made me feel like a number; she made me feel like an informed mother.

—**Juliet Zita**, Tax Preparer/Mom

After Jamey's first round of SAT and ACT testing, we learned that being a straight-A student does not necessarily translate into standardized testing excellence. We began a tutoring program with Valley Prep to ensure that when colleges reviewed her applications they wouldn't see a disconnect between her GPA and her test scores. Jamey achieved a 5-point increase on her ACT score, and acceptance into her dream school, Vanderbilt University. She will pursue her degree in elementary education with interdisciplinary studies in psychology. Her preliminary award for her freshman year was $52,000 in grants!

—**Nancy Gallegos**, Operations Manager/Mom

USC is in our family, and it was family tradition for my daughter to apply, but it made us nervous because we knew her writing skills needed strengthening. She is now a sophomore at USC and loves it. Trusting Pamela Donnelly was the right decision at the right time, and a really smart investment. No matter where the road leads, I know Natalie will always remember Ms. D as one of the pivotal influences of her teenage years.

—**Nora Gaghinjian**, Restaurant Owner/Mom

As a mother of two, I can only imagine the trepidation that lies ahead when the time comes for me to help my daughters navigate their journey into college. When it does, there is no one I trust more than Pamela Donnelly to be our guide. Not only does she offer solid strategies and important information, but her intuition as a mother and her deep heart are invaluable.

—**Marcia Cross**, Professional Actress (*Desperate Housewives*, *Melrose Place*)/Mom

From students:

Ms. D, thank you for believing in me academically and artistically. You are an incredible woman, teacher, mentor, and friend. Thanks to you and Valley Prep for being a key part in my educational journey, I am on my way to University of Miami in preparation to become an entertainment lawyer. I cannot even begin to express my genuine gratitude that I can now help protect other minor performers in the industry I've grown up loving. I feel so blessed to have you in my life.

—**Jennifer Cooke**, University of Miami, Pre-Law

I got into all 4 University of California schools I applied to, and even had a $48,000 scholarship offer. My Critical Reading and Writing skills on the SAT increased 28% as a direct result of Valley Prep's strategies. I can't wait to attend my #1 choice, UCLA, in the fall. Pamela Donnelly is an educator who honestly cares about the future of students and their long-term success. I'm now able to commit my life's work to solving the riddle of Alzheimer's Disease, which plagued my grandfather.

—**Kylie Rostad**, University of California, Los Angeles, Pre-Med

I'm not just a professional actress; I'm an aspiring college-bound student. When I'm not preparing for a role, I'm reading literature, working on essays, and mastering math concepts. My mom and I have been so glad to be working with Pamela Donnelly

and her staff at Valley Prep to help me achieve my academic goals. Working professionally while getting through high school isn't easy, but with the right support, I am really living my dream right now. I trust Valley Prep—they are the best at what they do, and they do it with heart.

—Saxon Sharbino, Professional Actress
(*Trust Me, Touch*)/High School Student

Thanks to Pamela Donnelly and her staff, my average section score on the SAT leaped. My essays improved. I got into 9 of the 11 schools I applied to! I am so excited to be attending my #1 choice, Sarah Lawrence College. I loved working with Pamela Donnelly and Valley Prep since they really get how it feels to be a teen with all this pressure. It really helped me achieve my goals to know that they understood me. I'm now aiming for a writing career and a great future working for a major magazine.

—Taylor Burke, Sarah Lawrence College, Journalism

4 KEYS
TO COLLEGE
ADMISSIONS
SUCCESS

*Unlocking the Gate to the
Right College for Your Teen*

PAMELA
DONNELLY

NEW YORK

4 KEYS TO COLLEGE ADMISSIONS SUCCESS
Unlocking the Gate to the Right College for Your Teen

Published in New York, New York, by Morgan James Publishing. Morgan James and The Entrepreneurial Publisher are trademarks of Morgan James, LLC.
www.MorganJamesPublishing.com

The Morgan James Speakers Group can bring Pamela Donnelly to your live event. For more information or to book an event, visit The Morgan James Speakers Group at www.TheMorganJamesSpeakersGroup.com.

Columbia is a trademark of Columbia University.
Dartmouth is a trademark of Dartmouth College.
Yale is a trademark of Yale University.
Princeton is a trademark of Princeton University.

A free eBook edition is available with the purchase of this print book.

ISBN 978-1-63047-211-5 paperback
ISBN 978-1-63047-212-2 eBook
ISBN 978-1-63047-213-9 hardcover
Library of Congress Control Number:
2014935771

CLEARLY PRINT YOUR NAME ABOVE IN UPPER CASE

Instructions to claim your free eBook edition:
1. Download the BitLit app for Android or iOS
2. Write your name in **UPPER CASE** on the line
3. Use the BitLit app to submit a photo
4. Download your eBook to any device

Cover Design by:
Chris Treccani

Interior Design by:
Bonnie Bushman

In an effort to support local communities, raise awareness and funds, Morgan James Publishing donates a percentage of all book sales for the life of each book to Habitat for Humanity Peninsula and Greater Williamsburg.

Get involved today, visit
www.MorganJamesBuilds.com.

Habitat
for Humanity®
Peninsula and
Greater Williamsburg
Building Partner

For my daughters
Hannah, Lily, and Annabel,
and for my mother Molly.
You are the 4 keys to my success.

SPECIAL THANKS

 Love is a verb, talk is cheap, and actions matter. I offer my sincere gratitude to the following people for their personal support, professional development, and/or inspiration.

Susan Armendariz
Randall Balmer, PhD
Bruce Barbour
Ray Barreth
Joel Bauer
Liz Benedict
Michael Berthold
Kevin Burke
Jonathan Cardinia
Cindy Chanin
Vicki Shoemaker Cloud
Travis Cody
Marcia Cross
Greg Daniel
Marc Devoe
Thelma Donnelly
David Garfinkel
David Guç
Stephen Hall

David Hancock
Matthew Hayutin
Peter Kaufman
Larry King
Nethaly Leddel
Dan Magnus
Marina Martins
Sam Mikhail
Becky Radant
Amanda Rooker
Pamela Russell
Tommy Shaw
Bessie Shoemaker
James R. Shoemaker Jr.
Tim Shoemaker
Christina Tobin
Dr. Jacinth Tracy, PhD
Simon Treselyan
Marianne Williamson

TABLE OF CONTENTS

| | Foreword | xv |
| Introduction: | How to Not Screw It Up | xviii |

Key #1—Cognitive Independence ... **1**

Chapter 1:	Changes	3
Chapter 2:	Collage	17
Chapter 3:	Crutches	31
	Bonus: Teenage Brain Development	40
	Checklist #1	50

Key #2—Emotional Independence ... **51**

Chapter 4:	Mentors	53
Chapter 5:	Goals	66
Chapter 6:	Stability	76
	Bonus: 12 Pillars of Personal Power	90
	Checklist #2	94

Key #3—Physical Independence ... **97**

| Chapter 7: | Appearance | 99 |
| Chapter 8: | Finances | 106 |

Chapter 9:   College Quest   121
               Bonus: How to Keep Your Teen   133
               Safe on Campus
               Checklist #3   138

Key #4—Spiritual Independence   **139**
Chapter 10:   Grace   141
Chapter 11:   Tools   152
Chapter 12:   Types   165
               Checklist #4   180
               Bonus: Send Your Student to College   182
               Without Going Broke

Conclusion: Euphoria   189
Addendum 1   Is College Necessary for Success Today?   191
Addendum 2   Education Reform   196
Addendum 3   A Call to Action   205

FOREWORD

Randall Balmer, PhD

Mine is hardly a household name, and so I open this Foreword with a brief recitation of my credentials. Since earning the doctorate at Princeton University, I have taught for the last thirty years in some of the nation's finest institutions of higher education, including four of the eight schools in the Ivy League.

I have held endowed professorships at both Columbia University and Barnard College, and I am currently the Mandel Family Professor in the Arts and Sciences at Dartmouth College.

At various times over the past three decades, I have taught as a Visiting Professor at Yale, Princeton, Northwestern, and Emory universities, and at the Columbia University Graduate School of Journalism. I have published more than a dozen books and written, produced, and hosted three television documentaries for PBS, one of which was nominated for an Emmy Award.

I am also an Episcopal priest and the father of two sons who graduated from Columbia.

None of my accomplishments in life would have been possible if not for the solid foundation of a liberal arts education. Although I am a proud product, and a passionate defender, of public schools, my college years by far were the most formative—as they are, I suspect, for most people.

I know that a good education, especially one grounded in the liberal arts, is priceless, not only for long-term financial returns—studies consistently show that college graduates earn more throughout their lifetimes—but for the even greater returns of an inquiring mind, a robust curiosity, and informed, responsible citizenship. A good college experience can—and should—encourage and develop those characteristics.

Besides, there are few pursuits more satisfying, in my judgment, than the life of the mind.

As a parent, I know that preparing your children for college, not to mention winning admission to that college, can be daunting. That is why I'm so impressed with this book. Pamela Donnelly has impeccable credentials as a summa cum laude graduate of one of the most prestigious universities in America, where she focused on her twin callings as an educator and author.

She is wise and witty and winsome—and I have seen firsthand that she is an exceptional mother as well. I'm proud to claim her as one of my former students, although I take no credit whatsoever for her brilliance. Her passion for education was as evident then as it is now, and your children are the ones who benefit.

Pamela's comprehensive approach to the college admissions process focuses on developing the whole person—Spiritual, Physical, Emotional, and Cognitive. I can think of nothing more crucial to success than attaining this balance, not only in college but also in life.

Preparing well-rounded children is one of the most important tasks we face as parents—and admissions staff members at top schools don't just want to see grades and scores. I've participated in enough committee and faculty meetings over the years to know that colleges are looking for well-rounded, fully dimensional human beings. They are looking for the skills and knowledge outlined here.

Pamela Donnelly provides invaluable guidance, which she has earned the old-fashioned way. Get ready to save yourself a steep learning curve by tapping into her wealth of knowledge; she offers a lifetime of experience in this collection of insightful essays.

HOW TO NOT SCREW IT UP

Trust yourself. You know more than you think you do.
—**Dr. Benjamin Spock**, Child Psychologist/Author

Dr. Spock was right. Raising a child comes to most parents naturally. When we do what comes instinctively, many aspects of parenthood just fall into place. The trouble is, by the time college applications loom on the horizon, many parents become stuck. They don't know how to strategically position their sons and daughters for success.

None of us mean to fall short, of course. It's just that, up until now, no one has pointed out that transitioning our kids through college admissions and into thriving lives requires four distinct keys. When you foster your son or daughter's cognitive, emotional, physical, and spiritual independence using the methods described in this book, you enable them to make the right choices. You catapult them toward the college of their dreams.

My intention is to show you through the lessons and outlines in this book what many parents have told me for years they've been looking to find—a comprehensive outline helping them usher their teenager out of the nest and into a bright future, both academically and personally.

It's funny. We use checklists for the simplest things, like buying groceries for a special menu. Forgetting the right spices for a pie seems pretty mundane compared to leaving out a needed ingredient for the recipe of effective parenting. But make no mistake—some of these rarely discussed missing ingredients are crucial. When we do not adequately prepare a child to become a successful young adult, the consequences will be far more serious and longer lasting than if we leave out nutmeg from the pumpkin pie for Thanksgiving.

I've personally seen the information detailed here help thousands of teens navigate one of the most challenging rites of passage in adult life, and that same knowledge can help your family, too.

Let's admit one thing here and now: helping our children from cradle to graduation can feel like a series of locked gates. None of us gets handed a big ring of keys when our babies are born, but we somehow find our way, year by year. We are simultaneously teacher and student. As we diaper our sons and daughters, eventually teaching them how to walk and then run, they teach us the most central lesson of life: how to love more deeply and unconditionally than ever before, and then, how to let go. I have yet to meet a mother or father who isn't determined to get this parenting thing right. We just need the strategies to get us there.

I counsel parents who work with my staff in Los Angeles to begin with the end in mind. That end result is not merely getting teens into the right college. Sure, that's often part of the plan, but college is a vehicle, not a destination. The true end result most parents long for is seeing their sons and daughters enjoying the personal and financial freedom to share their abilities and talents with a grateful world. Of course, this often *begins* with college. Because there are so many worthy callings in this life that do not require a college education, let's acknowledge that for some students a trade school (plumbing, electrical, cosmetology) is a more appropriate alternative. I know one young man who disliked school so much it troubled his parents terribly. He bypassed college to learn underwater welding, and now earns more money per hour than many college graduates — while repairing bridges wearing scuba gear. So, there are many ways our sons and daughters can find their independence. This book presumes you know that yours is college-bound, but I would be remiss not to acknowledge the many non-academic options out there.

So: the process described in this book culminates in an emotional tsunami as we drive away from dropping our babies off in a dorm for the first time. In the meantime, we often scramble for strategies. Where can we turn?

Shockingly enough, after 18 years of committed effort as moms and dads, a funny thing happens. We simultaneously celebrate loudly and inwardly grieve. Our babies are gone. At that point, all we can do is hope we have prepared them properly. One parent I know recently joked that this book should be handed out in every maternity ward in the country. I laughed, but in a way it made perfect sense. It never hurts to know what lies ahead, and it's never too early to prepare.

Here's a little reality check: if you're the parent of an incoming high school freshman you have exactly 180 weeks before they graduate. That's it. Done. Finito. A mere 45 months to be sure they are fully equipped. Look at how quickly time dwindles down:

	Months	Weeks	Days
Freshman	45	180	1,350
Sophomore	33	132	990
Junior	21	84	630
Senior	9	36	270

This list should evoke a combination of relief and urgency. The time is *now* to get strategic.

Nobody warns us about any of this when we are making googley-eyes at that future co-parent and foregoing birth control in our hormonal, pheromone-induced trance. Well, before you reach for the remote control to watch old episodes of *Family Ties*—where all of life's troubles for teens magically resolve within 23 minutes between commercials for Coke and pimple cream—take a deep breath and remember you are already in the home stretch. Your baby grew up. No more elementary school or even middle school. Congratulations! That light at the end of the tunnel is your teen's future. Now, let's help them get to that light with as much ease and excellence as possible.

No one would argue that adults should think their own thoughts, do their own laundry, vote their own consciences, and pay their own bills and taxes. But do we really expect this capacity for independence to magically and instantly happen on an arbitrary deadline, like an 18th birthday?

By the time our babies hit 13, some parents lapse into absolute nostalgia for the swaddled start of their little ones' lives. This is the humble pie that can choke you if you're not ready. Ah, those halcyon months of reading books and practicing Lamaze. Can your memory still conjure images of birthdays one, two, and three? As those candled cartoon cakes crumble into the past, the stakes get higher. It can feel really overwhelming (and if I didn't know that firsthand I'd have no business writing this book).

When we can anticipate the twists and turns of adolescence, we make informed choices in our responses to the bumps along the terrain. You may be in the thick of it, and feel so much pressure you want to throw this book on the floor in frustration over the behavior of your teenage son or daughter. If that's you, take heart. Realize that it is completely possible to help your teen forge a fantastic future, no matter how frustrating things get. I've seen lots of mayday situations turn for the best with the right support in place.

Keep reading, and these four keys will help you through the home stretch toward your child's eventual college career. You'll probably even want to lend this book to your friends (but I don't mind if you buy them their own copies). Just don't assume some enchanted fairy elsewhere in their lives—at their school or on a sports field—is going to wave a wand and college acceptance letters will magically appear. It doesn't work that way. Dear parent, it's up to you to help them. The good news is: you *can* do it and I will show you how.

Each new day calls us to remember that just as we are not in charge of that rising sun in the sky, we are not responsible for micro-managing our teens' choices. They are bound to make mistakes, and that's normal. *A smooth sea never made a strong sailor*, as my grandmother used to say.

As parents of teens, we learn to ebb and flow, to take things day by day. This doesn't constitute the full task, however. We also have to mindfully weave in those improvisational lessons each day. Each of the four keys that comprise this book can truly prepare our kids for the best possible chance at admission to the right college and a well-balanced life.

Suffice it to say, parenting teens is less a science or an art form than a craft. We must learn to think on our feet or get knocked off of them. Unlocking the potential of another human being is not for sissies, and these four keys challenge each parent differently. For some, the physical independence aspects come easily, but emotionally separating from the teen causes agony. For others, cognitive independence comes naturally, but the spiritual component of parenting has eluded them.

One way to begin reading this book is to ask yourself which of the four keys you think you've already got under control. Which area, for you, seems to need the most support? How can you look at the remaining amount of time in your home as an opportunity to fill in the gaps?

Let us run with perseverance the race marked out for us.
—Hebrews 12:1

I've always loved this quote from scripture—maybe it's because I was raised in a Christian home. I think the metaphors of "fighting the good fight" and "running the race" are really helpful as a mom. I'm not here to tell anybody what he or she should believe, but by way of introduction you should know what I believe. I honestly believe that each child comes to its parents as a gift from God. Our job is to not, as they say, screw it up.

If you're like me, you probably already take tremendous comfort in knowing you are not alone on this quest to perform your parenting responsibilities carefully. You try to surround yourself with positive role models.

I feel lucky to make my living working with teens and their families, because it brings me such joy. I'm convinced that all parents basically want the same things—we want our kids to find purpose in their lives. The trick is they need our help to make that happen.

When I educate well, I teach my way right out of a job. When the student no longer needs me, I have been successful. Not needing me is okay, because getting to know my former students as successful young adults validates the time I've invested. Similarly, our goal as parents is not to become obsolete, but rather to reframe the relationship. We want to see these kids independent, not codependent. College admissions staff members want to see the same thing—and that doesn't happen without a plan.

Since I am probably a bit further down the road than many of you, let me share with you how this has played out for me in my life with my firstborn. She is entering her late 20s as I write this, and I must confess to the cliché of having blinked while she went from a dimpled four year old to a competent adult overseeing national non-profit organizations. She graduated near the top of her class from a great university with her degree in psychology, and those four years were the vehicle that transported her toward a life where she creates positive change in the world through her work with animals and marginalized members of society. Now it's not about nagging her to do her homework or to clean her room (that chaotic room!). It's about actively listening for the areas where my help is still needed, and I'm always so relieved when it is.

What's new is that lately she asks me for things like offering feedback on her outline for a speech she's giving at a university about gender inequities in American media instead of helping her blow her little nose. I'm still the only mom she's got, and when she's facing tough times, sometimes my phone rings.

My two younger children are in the early years of high school as I write. So you can trust me when I tell you that I am still right there with you.

There are no shortcuts—Dr. Spock was right. We get out of it what we put in. To effectively unlock the gates to college admission to the right college for our teens is to know deep within our own hearts that we have given this child every advantage we had.

We may not be perfect, but our love is. For the rest of our lives, we will live with the results, for better or worse.

By the time we're done, this book promises to teach you how to get your teen to put down the cell phone long enough to actually talk with you, how to confidently navigate the college admissions process, and to show you how to teach them to set their inner compass for a future where they live by design, not by default.

Once that happens, we can give ourselves a shiny gold star and take a long vaycay. I'm thinking Tahiti—who's in?

Key #1

COGNITIVE INDEPENDENCE

Chapter 1

CHANGES

It takes courage to grow up and become who you really are.

—E. E. Cummings

If we were to try to summarize the entirety of the teenage experience, we could boil it down to one word: change. Physical changes are the most apparent, but others abound. Voices change. Attitudes change. Preferences change. And, necessarily, a parent's relationship to his or her teenager must change as well. Navigating these changes from grade 7 onward means that by the time most folks reach the college applications process, the family dynamic has radically shifted.

These next several chapters provide the first and most obvious key as you prepare them for college—unlocking your teen's

3

independence as a thinker. Seek to encourage creativity in the way they approach what they are learning. Help them to see past the mere conformity of this thing we reductively call "school," and celebrate them as they bring something new to the table beyond memorization and high test scores. The dialogue by the time they are approaching or in high school needs to truly ratchet up a notch. Here's how.

Promote Question-Asking, Not Just Answering

Many of us who now parent teenagers remember a certain TV ad well—the egg in the sizzling hot pan. "This is your brain," the voiceover explained. An image of a pristine raw egg in the shell filled the screen. "This is your brain on drugs," we were told, as the egg was cracked and spilled into the heat that would change it. Let's extrapolate this vivid image as we consider the gaps between teens and adults.

If we could imagine a similar ad, it might go something like this: "This is your brain," showing a multi-cloverleaf interchange in a major US city with cars zooming along in complex patterns. "This is your teenager's brain." Image? A large orange *Under Construction* sign over an incomplete series of roads. This image underscores perhaps the single most important component of developing academic excellence: possessing enough innate curiosity to ask questions to lead to one's own unique point of contact with the material. There is no highway to knowledge, only trails each student must blaze alone.

Curiosity hasn't received good press over the centuries, but an active academic mind gives birth to new perspectives. Students today need to be like curious cats or they risk lazing around passively, being fed predigested bits of meat and dutifully regurgitating upon command. Although the mania for standardized testing offers predetermined answers residing between answers A and E, rarely does actual wisdom hide there.

Quest for the Right Questions

Confusion is a word we have invented for an order which is not yet understood.

—Henry Miller

The tricky thing about seeking answers to questions is in knowing the right ones to ask. According to many great writers throughout the ages, it is critical that people not only seek answers to the questions they are able to think of to ask, but also to consider the very real possibility that deeper, more meaningful questions exist. Some of these may not even be on their radar yet. Henry Miller, for instance, lived a decade of his life abroad, inspiring some of his greatest work. People often have to wander far from the familiar to discover their potential, whether that travel is geographic or metaphorical.

This means allowing for the mystical implications of the unknown (and unknowable) to be overtly incorporated into our discussions with our teenagers. Letting them see that we too have traveled far, wrestled with angels and demons, and had to seek and knock before finding and entering, can reposition us not as penultimate sources of wisdom but rather fellow-journeymen through life.

An example of this commonly arrives in the mid-high school years, when students ask their parents what they think they should select as a major for college. This question seems to beg a finite list of possibilities, and indeed there are limits to the actual majors various universities will offer them. But dig a little deeper for the question embedded inside the question, and you will find layer upon layer of stratified inquiries: How should I be positioning myself for future career success? What financial independence can you help me attain through my academic choices? And perhaps most basic (yet paradoxically elusive) of all: what is my purpose in life?

Another example of a question masking larger inquiries is the famous teen lament, "What's the point?" Oftentimes, a discouraged high schooler—whether from a friendship gone awry or a failed exam—will spiral at what seems like a radical pace to the brink of desperation. When they ask questions like, "why should I care?" or "why does it even matter?" it is important for parents to move the conversation to physical action and engagement with the outside world. In truth, any human being—whether child, adult, or mercilessly straddling between the two—can be bitten by the despair bug.

Get them moving, get them talking, and redirect the conversation. What is the core of the matter? A little gentle probing usually reveals confusion about their appropriate role in one area of their lives or another. Hold emotional space; stand guard while helping them process the puzzles of life. Sometimes they don't need a solution anyway, they just need an ear, a shoulder, and room to ponder. Scratch your head with them if you really don't know. Nothing draws a teen closer to their parent than seeing the true humility of the human condition on display. Put away the super-hero cape. You're not fooling anyone anyway, and maintaining honesty will help your teen much more than feigning omniscience.

Guide Them toward Bloom's Taxonomy

The key to true cognitive independence paradoxically requires teens to see through the guise of the education system as it is currently organized. The corporate necessities of federal dollars, state mandates and local policies can all boil down to a race to nowhere, with students gathering information without necessarily benefitting from the process. They need help connecting the dots of the "what" and the "why."

In other words, it's not just that they know what happened in the Civil War, but why it matters, and by extension what its implications are for other situations and information they have considered. No, they probably won't be able to escape the dreaded standardized tests that have the current education system in a stranglehold, but at least we can help them resurrect some joy in their learning process.

Bloom's Taxonomy is a really helpful concept for students to know, as it provides a way of thinking about subject matter that describes levels of thought as resembling something like a staircase. Each stair describes a new level of comprehension of the material. All thinking, writing, and analysis are not the same.

Down on the lowest step is the "what?" As in: "What is being taught?" It's important to understand what is being taught, for instance to be able to regurgitate the plot of a novel or play. In math, the 'what' would be something like being able to correctly restate the Pythagorean Theorem. As we go up the staircase of understanding, though, it's not enough just to know the 'what'. In history class, for example, we want to understand not just who does things, when they happen, and what is happening. On a higher level we want our teens to understand how things are happening.

"How" is a major question that separates the average student from the rock star. "How" demands an elevated way of thinking about complex things. How are the structures that that author is using conveying his or her theme and character development? Being able to analyze those sorts of inquiries is crucial for ambitious thinkers. With almost x-ray vision, look at each new concept you see as if it were the blueprint of a house. How is it structured?

Then, on an even more elevated level (careful not to get a nosebleed way up here in the stratosphere) we can encourage our students to look at "why." Why is the theme what it is? The "why" is, in some cases, a rhetorical question, but it's tremendously thought provoking to ponder the "why" in all academic endeavors. Here's an example: why are all American students taught about the Civil War?

The Spielberg movie *Lincoln* boasts powerful performances by Daniel Day Lewis and Sally Field, but the real gem was a script that knew to ask the "why." Maybe that's why audiences and critics loved it so much. A topic we've all heard about so much it could have been boring, came to life. It's interesting that so many students can tell you "what" happened in the Civil War, but few can explain the "how."

How did the 13th amendment get passed? And, more importantly, why? In the film, Lincoln's relationship to his youngest son and his son's compassion for the African American people that were living under slavery were keys to answering this question of "why." The "why" trumps the "what" every time, and you will find that's true in most academic classes. Yes, you have to know the "what" first, but for heaven's sake don't let your teen just plop down on the bottom step and take a nap. Have them start climbing.

College admissions staff members vet applicants. They seek essays written by students who have thoughtfully climbed those stairs. As the competition gets more and more challenging year by year, merely understanding the "what" (and "where" and "when") is not going to cut it. Ask them how. How is that theory put together in math? How did things develop at a particular time in history? And then, when they're really ready for the big leagues, ask the most important question of all: "Why?"

Teach Academic Advocacy

Not only do parents need to encourage their teens to be questions askers within the classroom environment, but they need to encourage their teens to advocate for themselves with teachers, administrators, and even bosses at work with assertiveness and charm. By learning to be proactive now, they develop skills that will help them throughout their lives. Teens who never learn this skill are hindered indeed. How can you help?

- Role play scenes with you as the teacher and them asking for extra-credit options after class.
- Help them plan a series of specific questions for a one-on-one conference that they set up for themselves (hint: teachers love it when these are not just about raising grades, but about expressing interest in the material and a desire to learn more through newly recommended books, articles, etc.).
- Help them to understand the fine line between appropriate subordination with a boss and being too fearful to speak up about concerns in the workplace.
- Brainstorm other opportunities with coaches, pastors, and other adults to find and showcase their voice,

especially in situations where disagreement or conflict could arise.

Until teens become able to self-advocate in a world of adults, they will remain complicit or inadvertently silenced and disempowered. The time to help them practice these crucial skill sets is before they need them in college.

Raise Politically Conscious Teens

Parents should aim to get their kids involved in active American citizenship long before they turn 18. Although some colleges tend to lean more left or right, few espouse an ostrich approach to current events. Get them reading the news—even if just on Sundays or online. Help them notice the subjective slant of various news organizations. Ask them if they understand why Al Gore didn't become president in 2000 despite winning the popular vote. By the time your son or daughter is of voting age, several years may have passed since they had government as part of their coursework at school. Help them remember, or teach them for the first time, how the Electoral College, caucuses, delegates, and other key factors work together in an American election. Depending on the intended major, some college admissions interviews may veer toward political topics. Be sure they're aware.

As long as you and other key adults in their lives are engaged in the political process, they are more likely to follow suit. From infancy to 4th grade, I raised my firstborn in Manhattan. I vividly remember walking with her from our brownstone on West 88th Street on the Upper West Side to a church by the horse stables at Claremont on West 89th. The voting volunteers would often make jokes about the "little voter" and allow her to come into the booth with me. I would show her the index card on which

I'd written my selected candidates and votes for resolutions in preparation to pull those cool levers she liked.

These days my firstborn isn't politically active in an identical way to me, but I can tell you that around the time of Occupy Wall Street she was involved in a protest that shook me to my core. My precious little girl, who had so proudly worn her Mommy's "I Voted" red, white, and blue sticker each election in New York City, was shoved to the concrete by a police officer when she and a group of her peers were peacefully protesting in Chapel Hill, much to my horror. It was on the evening news.

Thank goodness she wasn't injured, but I have to believe that knowing she had the right to her voice, to be heard even in protest, came in some measure from seeing her mother active politically throughout her young life. Although it was a terrifying experience for me as a mother, I confess that I felt proud. She has never been a "monkey see, monkey do" kind of person, but if she learned not to stay silent by watching me express my voice, all I can say is hooray.

There is an important distinction between discussing political matters with a teen and forcing them to think the way we do. Just like they have the right to determine their own faith walk, or lack thereof (see Key #4, Spiritual Independence, later), they also have the right to join a different political party or see cultural issues through a unique lens. If you really want to anger or alienate them, be a bully.

Watching debates, press conferences, and inaugural speeches with your teen provides a great opportunity to share in the public discourse. "Why is everyone standing up?" I can remember my daughter asking while watching Bill Clinton's State of the Union address many years ago. Instead of answering, I gave her a question in return, "Why do you think?" It can be fascinating to hear how a younger pair of eyes views something you might assume has only one possible interpretation.

If your teen is particularly drawn to the political realm, be sure to cultivate those tendencies with leadership opportunities such as school clubs, class elections, and sports teams. These experiences help teens develop leadership skills and give context for seeing themselves as agents for change within the larger social structure. Debate club and forensics are terrific aptitude builders for critical thinking, persuasion, and the art of rhetoric.

When the time comes to register them to vote, be sure they know they can either do it online or by going to the local post office. Only 50% of the eligible voters under 24 years old were registered to vote in 2000, and although that number has improved it is still a far cry from ideal.

Since an 18th birthday is seen by so many in our society as the major tripwire between childhood and adulthood, sending forth a young American without a political compass is lazy at best and reckless at worst. We can do better, and establishing a foundation for political involvement can help your teen and the world around them.

Rock the Vote

When Rock the Vote first began appealing to teens and college students in 1990, the political apathy of an entire generation had spurred founder Jeff Ayeroff to do something about it. Certainly, no American adult can be seen as truly independent in the context provided by our Founding Fathers without active participation in our democratic process. In 2012, 19% of the voters who put Obama back in the White House were 18 to 29 years old. The trend has been slowly moving upward, since in 2008 that number had been 18%. This begs the questions: Why should parents care if their teens vote, and what does it have to do with preparing them for college?

The future of this country rests in the hands of the American people. Anyone who has studied world history will attest that people's lives are intensely impacted by the political systems in place—think of the Russian, French, or Glorious Revolutions. People riot and die when governments reel out of control. It matters to your teen's future welfare that the right candidates are placed in office. And it matters to you.

One challenge with teens is that their peers may be disconnected from the political world, and see it as the realm of old stuffy men on Sunday morning channels that they fly past on their way to the latest episode of a favorite TV show. One key to engaging your teen's curiosity is to stay connected yourself, and feed digestible sound bites of info to them throughout the week—at dinner, on the way to ball practice, etc. Have the news on when they come in the door from rehearsal, and let them hear you reacting to what Congress just did, or a speech by the president. Whether you agree or disagree, letting them see you as an involved citizen sets the stage for them to become one too. They might not say anything in particular ("Gee, mother, thank you for enlightening me" will probably not spring from their lips). But that doesn't mean they're not listening and likely to emulate you.

Many cultural issues matter to teenagers on a very personal level. Making the political personal is one great strategy to get them engaged. Here are some key examples:

- **Education.** Does their school have enough funding for the arts and other programs like music? What government policies will dictate which college they can attend? On local, state and federal levels, there are school boards and teacher's unions impacting their options.

- **Ecology.** Do your teens enjoy breathing oxygen? Really? Perhaps now is the time to consider how US fiscal policies are driving ecological shifts that will impact both their lives and those of your great-grandchildren. Are oceans and clean drinking water important? These are political issues, whether anyone likes it or not. Ignorance is not bliss.

- **Discrimination.** Can your teen get the job he or she wants without racial profiling, gender bias, or other insidious stereotype-driven limitations? How much do they understand about Affirmative Action and other federal programs, and do they recognize the voters' power to impact those rules?

- **Media.** Censorship makes teens angry, but some of their favorite music genres are frequently banned. Do they understand the right to free speech and other amendments and constitutional provisions for their lives in the "land of the free?" Caution: expecting their history teacher at school to handle this is a cop-out. Even though the classroom can give them background, their ability to plug that information into the now in large part rests upon you and the example you set. Do they understand the role of the FCC, filters on the World Wide Web, etc.? How do they feel about the NSA reading their supposedly private text messages, email, tweets, and Facebook postings? Do they realize that many college admissions staff members consider searching and viewing social media postings by applicants as fair game? (A word to the wise: be sure they go back through their online history and clean it up. I've heard too many stories where photos incongruent with a school's values sabotaged an otherwise strong application.)

- **Money.** Money matters. A lot. Teens know it and so do we, but in terms of their perceived reality, this is not about macro or microeconomics, it is about money for a used car to get to and from college, or a tank of gas. Help them see the national debt as a real problem their generation is inheriting and will have to solve. Money is not just personal; it is political. (Why do so many dead presidents adorn our bills?)

- **Equality.** Your teen may or may not be directly affected by the matter of gay rights, but you can bet there are others in his or her peer group who are. What role do they want their government to play in handling ethical issues like equality and religious freedoms? (Do they understand the difference between freedom of religion and freedom from it?)

- **Abortion.** Pro-life? Pro-choice? If they don't vote, they need to clam up. Do they really want to leave such a vital issue in the hands of other voters?

Let's recognize that teens need reminding that their votes can change laws that matter—laws that could affect them and their friends. Resources like www.vote-smart.org give bipartisan breakdowns of all the candidates and their perspectives on a federal, state and even local level to help voters make informed decisions before they go to the polls. Organizations like www. freeandequal.org are working to move the dialogue beyond two parties and toward more independent candidates seeking and attaining office. This fascinating time in our political landscape merits the attention of all college-bound teens.

Chapter 2

COLLAGE

Every child is an artist. The problem is how to remain an artist once we grow up.

—Pablo Picasso

Connect the Dots

Remember, when your kid was in kindergarten, all those art projects that came home by the arms full? I lost count of how many magazine images were torn and carefully glued to honor various themes of the week. What was really smart about all that collage work was that, in essence, those types of projects provide the framework for what needs to come later for inspired thinking. What does ripping up little bits of paper have to do with teaching teens to be cognitively independent as they approach the college years?

Merriam-Webster's Dictionary defines *collage* in several ways:

- **a** : an artistic composition made of various materials (such as paper, cloth, or wood) glued on a surface
- **b** : a creative work that resembles such a composition in incorporating various materials or elements <the album is a *collage* of several musical styles>
- **c** : a work (as a film) having disparate scenes in rapid succession without transitions

Just as a collage is the art of overlapping images from seemingly disparate sources, brilliant teen thinkers learn to collate, compare and contrast material from inside, outside, and nowhere near "the box." They do what my favorite verb of all time describes (yes, oftentimes we geeky teacher types actually have favorite verbs, and this one is mine). They *juxtapose*.

When students recognize the fact that they are not merely being asked to "fill a bucket" of facts, they come alive. I've seen it again and again. Some teens just "get it"—their body language in the classroom, interactions with their teacher, and written responses all reflect personal investment. In order for teens to build this fire inside themselves, though, parents and mentors need to stoke the embers. By modeling for them and encouraging them to follow as we mentally rearrange the pieces of information in new and even random ways, the interconnectivity frequently leads to inspiring school work and personal growth.

Let me give you an example. A certain AP Art History teacher I know loves to help students see the connections between the paintings and architecture of an era and the history they already know from social studies classes. These teens end up wanting to compare the scientific developments, religious beliefs, and literature of those time periods as well, and become animatedly engaged. Those interconnections provide a vital point of access for teens both in terms of not only academics but also their burgeoning worldviews.

This teacher recounted how one young man's eyes sparkled as he recognized the fact that during the high Renaissance Leonardo da Vinci created *artistic* works informed by *scientific* investigation—from "The Last Supper" to the "Mona Lisa" and "Vitruvian Man." He pondered da Vinci's incorporation of the sciences of physiology and anatomy into his art. He wrote a terrific essay about da Vinci's philosophy—how as a Christian he was inclined to see science and art merely as different paths leading to the same destination—a higher spiritual truth.

In truth, both teens and adults find this stuff fascinating when they are invited to seek the connections across cultures and the great divide of (supposedly separate) school subjects. Interestingly, da Vinci's biography attests that his father, a prominent notary, secured for him an apprenticeship at age 15 to the leading artist of Florence during the early Renaissance. Dear old dad did something very right there. By securing for his son the right mentor at the right age, a legacy of treasures remains that the world still enjoys today. Let's all encourage our teens to notice that everything they encounter, whether in school or outside of it, is interconnected. The "aha" of connectivity can mean the difference between joy and boredom.

Students who know to ask questions, make connections, and make "collages" out of these "ripped pieces" of information ascend to new heights academically. Ironically, the actual art form of collage didn't come into vogue until 1912 when Pablo Picasso pasted a section of commercially printed oilcloth to his Cubist painting, "Still Life with Chair Caning." Picasso breaks up the figure and objects in the style known as Cubism.

Instead of showing things as distinctly recognizable forms, he paints them from several points of view. Teens benefit by considering the metaphor here—when we try to simultaneously embrace multiple perspectives of any person, place, event, or thing we enhance our understanding of it. Similar to da Vinci's ability to sustain a broad perspective across multiple disciplines, I've seen students genuinely intrigued by the realization that Picasso's work at the beginning of the 20th century parallels Einstein's theory of relativity, which asserts the contingent nature of observing reality.

The key of cognitive independence unlocks this rather radical concept: although schools create separations and lists and "subjects of study," these constructs are actually somewhat arbitrarily separated. The sooner teenage students can grasp the truth that human experience is one big interconnected puzzle— whether in words, buildings, paint, events, or collage—the closer they get to unlocking the right future.

School Breaks: Initiate, Don't Vegetate

The collage of a well-organized series of events on a teen's calendar provides another important opportunity for parents who want to give their children the right support. Teens need enrichment like gardens need fertilizer. By the time they've completed a full year of schoolwork, those ten weeks of summer vacation can feel like a well-earned time to watch You Tube and work on a tan. But parents need to guide their kids as they try to develop the same inner balance that adults must strive to create—the correct amount of play to balance all that work.

Of course, summer is a time for beaches and barbecues and sleeping late sometimes. The problem is that many parents allow their teens to go from 75 mph to a screeching halt. After moving through final exams, proms, and the excitement of friends graduating ahead of them they sometimes want to remove their batteries in favor of sofa surfing and mental coagulation. It's not their fault—they honestly are exhausted, and deserve some time to catch their breath. They just don't need ten full weeks to do that.

College admissions staff members don't expect students to hold full time jobs while curing cancer and solving political tensions in the Middle East between June and September, but a summer filled with nothing constructive to report has created admissions hurdles for more than a few teens I've mentored over the years. Parents seeking to turn the key to cognitive independence need to initiate dialogue about the summer to come starting no later than 8th or 9th grade. March/April, around spring break, is a good time to try to nail a few things down. In fact, waiting longer than that will sometimes mean lost opportunities in a few of the six primary areas I recommend you consider. Not all students should implement all six of these, but all students will benefit by including at least a few of them.

The Art of the A+ Summer

Volunteer

Teenagers are not toddlers, and need adults to teach them that the world needs each of us to give back, not just take. Encourage them to find at least one community service commitment, whether once a week, for a weekend, or longer. Some teens I've known have gathered valuable work and leadership experience by being junior counselors at camps for disadvantaged youth, helping with concessions at Special Olympics, or just stocking grocery bags for their area food pantry for the homeless. Nonprofits like soup kitchens and animal shelters frequently seek volunteers, and depending on the teen's interests and intended major in college (if known), this is a great time to target not only real-world experiences but also potential reference letters from community members who can vouch for the contributions and character of the teen on letterhead stationery.

Work

Paid employment holds a special appeal for many teens, and understandably so. Seasonal employment over summer breaks gives many an opportunity to experience generating their own income for the first time in their lives. This can be heady stuff, and dovetails nicely with the race for physical independence (see the chapter on finances in section three). Common options include hometown parks, community centers, and schools for younger kids. While working in a leadership position is ideal, even something like working on a staff at a local business can generate essay ideas for future college prompts. For example, I worked at our hometown swimming pool as a lifeguard and swim coach the summer before my senior year, and the process of learning how to pass my water safety instructor test eventually led me to recognize my calling as an academic teacher. Colleges want to be able to see how you became you. Jobs you've worked and lessons learned there can provide a great framework for all of that.

Travel

Not everyone can afford to fly to Paris and Dubai every summer, but most American families can look for some sort of travel option to expand students' horizons — even if it is a road trip across the state. Of course, actually exploring foreign countries will exponentially expand your teen's awareness of other cultures, not to mention helping them hone their language skills. (*Dónde está el cuarto de bano, por favor?* Suddenly this phrase becomes more pressing when in Spain or Puerto Rico and needing to use the bathroom.)

Another form of travel meriting mention here is the all-important college visit. Campus visits, preferably by grade 10 but definitely by grade 11, should be part of the summer plans of every teen who plans to go to college and can afford the travel costs. Colleges love to hear that applicants were checking them out early in their high school careers, and including this in interviews or essays at application time can set them apart from other applicants.

Take Classes

Many high schools, both in person and online, offer summer classes. This can help teens recover from a D or lower on a final report card by retaking a class, or advance their math or language skills (hint: try to get to Calculus by senior year if you can, and four years of foreign language looks way better than two or three, no matter what your high school "required"). Local community colleges also offer for-credit summer courses and allow high school juniors and seniors to enroll. What a great way to divvy up courses in anticipation of easing the transition into freshman year of college.

I've seen smart parents start their teens as early as 10th grade taking two core curriculum classes each summer (English 101 or Intro to College Math, for example—two common prerequisites). By the time they graduate high school, they are well on their way to sophomore status—especially if they took AP courses and are attending a college that accepts those for college credit (note: many don't anymore). Another great thing about this option is that it is a way teens can explore possible career options while their schedules are still pliable enough to modify in the event they find a passion. Many organizations also offer fun enrichment activities that aren't actual classes, but still provide academic enrichment that looks great on college applications: creative writing workshops, scientific symposia, engineering conferences, and more. Do some research online, but do it early (usually by mid-April, almost always by late May) before missing deadlines.

Prepare for Testing

Standardized tests are a necessary evil, and for juniors who haven't hit adequate scores on the SAT or ACT, the summer between junior and senior year is a time to double down on some tutoring and study time to increase those numbers. Once you've helped your teen look online to determine 8 to 10 colleges of interest (a few safety schools with low requirements, several target schools that feel within reach, and a few long shots are often recommended) gather data on college website admissions pages or by calling to determine their average score accepted in the previous year's candidate pool. If your scores are more than 10% below that mark, it may be time for a retake in the fall of the senior year. Summer is great for this, too, because teen brains aren't already fried from homework and other school activities.

Play Sports

Playing on intramural teams, community leagues, or with school organizations can give athletic teens a real advantage, not just physically but cognitively (all that blood flow and oxygen works wonders for the mind's acuity). There are even potential financial benefits for those who may be scholarship candidates in a sport, if they perform well in tournaments or competitions—whether in tennis, golf, gymnastics, or on team sports. College admissions boards don't like "one trick pony" students, though, so be certain that sports activity is balanced with other categories outlined here. If your kid could be considered a "jock," guard against letting them be miscategorized as "dumb" by filling out some of their summer with social, mental, and altruistic activities.

New Majors for a New Millennium

Specialization and entrepreneurship are what's happening now. Antiquated models are churning out too many college graduates qualified for fields that are dwindling, while the true needs aren't met because so many parents are in the dark about aiming their teens toward the right things. Effective parents know their college-bound students need to consider new majors for the new millennium in order to be successful in the world they will inhabit.

Don't assume it's like it was "back in the day." Face it, we each only know what we know based on experiences, presumptions and prejudices of an era long gone by the time our teens are approaching college age. My daughters look at me with a mixture of disbelief and horror when I tell them that there were no such things as personal computers when I graduated high school in 1980. As someone who learned to type on an old-school ribbon typewriter (carbon copy paper, anyone?) I would be at quite a disadvantage in guiding my teens today to their futures if I hadn't evolved with the times—from my first clunky desktop computer in the mid-80s to the sleek Macbook Pro on which I now type this chapter. This ain't our grandma's era anymore—we've come a long way, baby, so let's get informed about where the trends are taking teens and advise them accordingly.

According to *US News and World Report* in September 2012, here are several of the most up and coming unexpected majors with expansive potential for job placement after college, as well as significant financial rewards once in the coveted positions that are opening up in the current marketplace. Parents take note: don't pay tens of thousands of dollars to get a degree for your kid that still won't pay their bills and fund some thrills. Life's too short, and you've worked too hard for that money. Here are what I call the Lucky Seven—for now, anyway. This moving target will no doubt change over time:

1. Biomedical Engineering

If your kid shows strength in science, this is a great area to explore—biomedical engineers combine engineering science and technology to come up with fixes for everything from preventing cancer, to inventing medical devices, engineering medications, and even designing surgical robots. The US Bureau of Labor Statistics says between 2008 and 2018, this field will have a 72% rate of job growth. Sounds good, right? Bonus: bragging rights that "my kid is helping mankind."

2. Computer Game Design

When I was growing up we had Pong. My brother and I would sit on a shag carpet in our living room and watch two white rectangles bounce a blipping square "ball" across a vertical "net." When Mario and Luigi came out years later, it seemed like something out of a science fiction movie to me. Over the past several decades I've seen students so obsessed with Halo and Call of Duty it can only be described as addiction—one sophomore's parents literally had to take the machine to work with them because he was failing classes to play compulsively. No surprise, then, that colleges now offer majors in game design for an industry expected to reach $82.4 billion (yes, that's a B, not an M) globally by 2015.

Games are not just for play anymore, as our culture has adapted these protocols for training our military, firefighters, corporate workers, and more. Jobs include game production, development, design, art, programming, computer graphics, and human computer interaction. Those who specialize as software engineers also find great jobs in architecture, medicine, law, and other industries using interactive simulation. So notice: if they want to go old school and "become a doctor or a lawyer"—this area of expertise can allow them a strong placement within those industries without the hands-on blood and guts of being a surgeon or having to pass the LSAT.

3. Environmental Studies
People across the globe are awakening to human impact on our shared natural resources. From energy to water, food, and climate concerns, environmental studies is a major with major importance for all of us, and incorporates that idea of collage. By taking interdisciplinary classes in health, food, agriculture, energy, biodiversity, climate, history, culture, land use, and public policy, students learn how to make every day Earth Day and often find satisfying career paths as a result.

4. Health Information Management
As the American population ages and more and more of us are living longer, increased numbers of workers are needed to manage information systems related to improve health and manage payments. Courses can include biomedical core courses—anatomy, physiology, and medical terminology—along with basic computer courses, management information systems, and

systems analysis and design. The American Medical Informatics Association projects a need for more than 50,000 workers in the next five to seven years. If your teen would feel happy in an office environment supporting those in the medical field, this is a good fit. Like computer game design, this major allows participation in healthcare without needing malpractice insurance.

5. Homeland Security

Living in a post-9/11 America, there is little surprise to see this one on the list. There are now over 75 college programs leading to undergraduate degrees focused on this specialization. Courses offered by many schools include critical infrastructure, criminal justice, emergency and disaster planning, weapons of mass destruction, and constitutional issues in homeland security. This is a great fit for patriotic teens who may have an interest in police work minus the need for the bulletproof vest that can make moms nervous. Some jobs may be with the US government, allowing for great benefits in terms of medical insurance, retirement packages, etc. Other positions may be with subcontracting agencies, but still offer high levels of job stability. Yes, it is both interesting and ironic that our nation's insecurity can spell job security for teens. By the way, cyber-security is another aspect of this field, and employs increasing numbers of college graduates with the right degrees and certifications. Classes involve technical aspects of protecting computer systems, networks, and individual computers. With all the viruses and villains out there, these careers can pay top dollar.

6. Nanotechnology

This industry is so new many parents today have no idea what it is, and yet it's poised to grow to $2.4 trillion worldwide by 2015 and employ 2 million people in this country by 2020. Basically, it's all about microscopes and teensy weensy particles that impact the usefulness, safety, and excellence of everything from golf clubs and skis, to car parts, dental implants, buildings and bridges. (Talk about versatile, right?)

This is another major in the new millennium that relates to the field of medicine without your kid wearing a stethoscope, since nanotechnology-based medicines are being used to treat cancers. Another overlap exists with the environmental sciences in that current researchers seek more energy-efficient fuel cells, solar panels, batteries, and environmental cleanup techniques. As long as your student loves science and has great eyes with good vision for staring at all those little microbes and molecules, this is an under-populated area of study with a wide field of job opportunity.

7. New Media

More and more colleges in recent years have begun offering courses and majors in what is broadly referred to as "new media." What does this mean? They combine communications and journalism curricula with offerings in digital media and design. MIT, for example, offers a Comparative Media Studies program, and USC now offers a BA in Interactive Entertainment. Students at USC combine a liberal arts background with a specialization in cinematic arts such as filmmaking, writing, and directing.

College degrees in new media prepare students for creative careers in filmmaking, television, animation, social media, e-text and Web publication, graphic design, and audio and visual arts. Whereas twenty years ago a simple one-size-fits-all approach worked well for college students interested in careers as creative writers, artists, and designers, today's technologies redefine the skill sets needed to succeed in the real world of those industries.

The wrong major can land your kid at the bottom of the stack of resumes when hiring time comes.

❖———————❖———————❖

Here's the bottom line on new majors: parents need to remember to guide teens to careers, not just colleges. How can you envision with your student individuated and self-driven ways to collate and combine multiple areas of interest? In doing this mindfully and successfully, you position them to become the only logical choice for a future boss looking to hire someone in one or more of these related fields.

Chapter 3

CRUTCHES

That's been one of my mantras—focus and simplicity. Simple can be harder than complex: You have to work hard to get your thinking clean to make it simple. But it's worth it in the end because once you get there you can move mountains.

—Steve Jobs

I n order to see clearly, we need to remove false perceptions and the dingy lens of limitations. The irony of Steve Jobs's quote notwithstanding, the crutches upon which many Americans rely today may impede what might actually serve them at a higher level. We don't want to send our kids off to college with the disadvantage of limited focus and concentration.

Technology: Device or Vice?

Few American parents would argue that technology has a death grip around the necks of their teenage students. According to the Nielsen Company, the "typical" teen sends and receives 3,417 text messages per month. That averages more than seven per waking hour. And let's not forget that these devices—the ubiquitous cell phone that dangles like an appendage from most teenagers with the means to own one—has replaced their teddy bears and baby blankies as their not-so-cuddly electronic pal. One in four teens reportedly are awakened at night by a text or email, and more than half of those attempt to read and/or answer it before resuming attempts to do something as mundane (but critical) as actually sleep. Disturbing.

Social media has exploded in the teen landscape, creating terrifying new stakes in the virtual realm. Chat room bullies and Facebook cruelty are concepts that current parents never had to face, fortunately for us. The inherent narcissism that teens are often accused of takes on truly menacing proportions when the I-Me-My obsessions of most social tweeting and status updating are considered. Even the dinner table, once the quiet respite at the end of a long day of school and work, and been infiltrated and hijacked by the ever-present cell.

How does this all play out in the classroom? In his book *Rewired: The Psychology of Technology,* Dr. Larry Rosen reports that students in 2012 were only able to focus and stay on task for an average of three minutes at a time. The number-one culprit for their distractions was technology. The internal hunger for social acceptance looms large in middle and high school, and therefore the need to check how many people have "liked" a new profile picture can feel important, even urgent. The fear of missing out on something compels compulsive behaviors that truly derail sustained cognition.

Life is, of course, filled with distractions, and that is as old as time itself. Learning to navigate both internal and external interruptions is one of the hallmarks of maturity. The concept of "metacognition" is defined as thinking about thinking. Teenagers who know how the brain functions often increase their ability to concentrate. Although some students are able to prioritize even when they see a text or Facebook message come in on their phones, others are less able to do so. This gap may explain the difference between those mature enough to delay gratification in the interest of better focus (and therefore grades) and those whose own inner distractibility quotient imperils them with the siren call of misused or overused technology.

So, is technology the student's friend or foe? The answer depends on whether it is their servant or master.

Despite the allure of shallow, skimmed information on the web, can all that dim sum sampling ever compare to a rich meal of deeply investigated and digested linear thought processing? Consider the fact that the human brain relies on neurons with somas that extend their tentacle-like axons and dendrites to send and receive impulses. That is what we are describing when we refer to the "instant gratification" of, say, a compulsive gambler walking into a casino. The brain wants that stimulation. Social media "addiction"—a concept I hear more and more parents lamenting in their students—can compromise the brain's willingness to sustain focus, academically and in other areas of life.

Ever since the Stone Age, humankind has sought ways to bring the outer world's experiences into accord with the inner landscape of the mind. Nowadays, according to some experts, we might as well begin writing a eulogy for the printed language. Even in places as sacrosanct as churches, parishioners are sometimes encouraged to bring their laptops to take notes on the sermon, or to Tweet from their pews about upcoming events. A typical public library bears witness to this metaphoric and literal shift—many layouts now proudly boast computer stations and electronically wired cubicles as the central hub, with printed books lying in the outer regions like a castaway tribe of trolls. Books are becoming nostalgic. Who'd have thought that was possible?

Reading has historically provided a central mode of communicating information, both in and out of classrooms. It is interesting to note that no spaces separated the words in early forms of writing. The extra cognitive burden of having to interpret separation allowed the act of reading to be more akin to a puzzle than it is today. Unlike the brains of animals, mankind had to develop a particular type of mental discipline in order to master the environment as we see today. With the advent of the Kindle, the Nook, and online e-texts, the idea of "reading a book" may be at risk of becoming a quaint anachronism. Major book chains close, and students increasingly rely upon digital vehicles to transmit curricular information. Why buy a novel, when it is free online at the push of a few keystrokes?

From the front lines, I can report that capitalism is alive and well in exploiting this trend among teens. I have seen students endeavoring to access poetry on a web page (or worse, cheat-sheet information on numerous websites devoted to quick, shallow summaries of complicated texts) deal with incessant pop-up ads for everything from face cream to dating services. By 2008, reading printed works was down 11% from 2004 among teens, and rates have continued in decline. Perhaps we should be happy for this. After all, think of all the saved ink, not mention the trees. Neither cedars nor pines are harmed in the digital transmission of text.

However, there is an increasing amount of data that suggests that the mode of delivery of the information does color the perception of the reader.

The "skimming" nature of computer usage inclines the human mind to minimal engagement with the material. Even the *New York Times* has embraced this trend. Beginning in March 2008, it began devoting three pages of each edition to brief synopses of events rather than the more in-depth reporting upon which it has predicated its reputation. In his insightful book *The Shallows*, Pulitzer Prize nominee Nicholas Carr quips, "We don't see the forest when we search the web. We don't even see the trees. We see twigs and leaves."

Contemplate, Don't Merely Juggle

The Internet alters brain function—this has been proven in lab studies that evaluate the impact of repetitive, intensive, interactive (dare I say addictive?) stimuli. The upshot is this: the Net seizes human attention, and then scatters it. The true danger here is that the imperative for students to develop their own inner voice, inner compass, and inner purpose in life is thwarted by the random mindlessness of a typical teen Internet session. The winds blow and away they go, often without noting or calculating the loss of their own forward momentum. It is as if they cease "swimming through life" and begin to tread water. A steady diet of that and it's time to call the Coast Guard. Eventually, students must progress or intellectually flounder.

The stark reality is that intellectual growth requires encoding smaller and larger bits of information into collated and synthesized thought patterns. The Internet's inability to regulate the amount of information being conveyed at a time makes it a less than ideal vehicle for communication, assuming the goal is long-term retention and integration. Unless the student prints out what they are reading, perhaps highlighting it or in some other way manipulating what is being read, the dynamic easily lapses into an "in one ear and out the other" exercise. Think about it: how many things you've read online over a month ago could you now cite with any accuracy?

Is contemplation becoming a lost art? Dr. Jordan Grafman, the head of the cognitive neuroscience unit at the National Institute of Neurological Disorders and Stroke, has been publically quoted saying there is a reverse correlation between increased ability to multitask and decreased ability to reflect upon matters deeply and creatively. What is gained in multiple tasks is lost in deliberateness of purpose. The result? A tendency to conform to predigested solutions and perspectives rather than originating one's own point of view. This is fine—assuming the goal is to create a race of robots, not people.

IQ scores have undergone interesting changes during the computer era. In 1992, 12th graders had a literary reading aptitude 12% higher than in 2005 according to the US Department of Education. The correlation between the increase of time students spent online and their decreasing critical reading skills is a cause for major concern among educators.

I read one educational theorist who compared the impact of Google as the intellectual equivalent of strip mining. The undue process of taking only relevant content in sound bites and disconnected pieces has replaced a slower "excavation" of actual relevance and meaning. So, rather than developing the necessary skill of intuition and internal wrestling for meaning, students now often settle for the cheap substitute of neurons firing and gratification being handed to them like a cheeseburger at a drive-through window.

In fact, ART—Attention Restoration Therapy—says that time spent in nature and away from technology allows cognition to improve due to the brain relaxing and therefore becoming both calmer and sharper. What effective parents know is that technology is a tool, not a tyrant. We must caution our teenagers about the perils of not developing intellectual skills away from that flickering screen.

Then again, there are benefits to technology in the educational system. When I was in high school, there were no such things as personal computers in my little hometown of Manassas, Virginia. Oh, I had heard of computers, sure. They were those big boxy things at NASA, filled with gadgets that calculated routes to Mars and important things like that.

In the early 1970s, not only did I consider Pong the height of technology—I took "keyboarding class" and learned to type on an old fashioned typewriter, complete with carbon paper and whiteout on a ribbon. My mother, who is now connected to her children and grandchildren on Facebook, was once a legal secretary and still knows how to take dictation in shorthand. Perhaps I should credit her with setting such a great example of rolling with the changes. Love you, Mom!

Thirty-plus years later: students working with my company now create PowerPoint presentations on laptops I could have never conceived of existing when I was their age. Our tutors mentor students on film projects shot on iPhones and edited in iMovie. They set these films to clips of songs from iTunes for project grades. Teachers in America access textbooks online every day –they research online, and use e-texts of classic novels, Shakespearean sonnets and Virginia Woolf essays.

Skype and iChat have further revolutionized options for students. The technology of built-in cameras and free Internet access to seeing and hearing one another in real time allows teachers and tutors to introduce a lesson on the weekend, and midweek do a review the night before a quiz to answer any questions and ensure students' maximum performance the next day. Many use white dry-erase boards behind them, and for all intents and purposes the student might as well be sitting in a classroom in a big expensive private school (one that their parents paid tens of thousands of dollars a year for them to attend, and that cost dozens of dollars in gas a day for transportation to and from the facility, plus another several hundred for uniforms and fees). In this scenario, students can wear their coziest jeans and sweatshirt, pet their favorite cat or dog on their lap, and learn what they need to know in the comfort of their own homes. Bonus: they can even wear fuzzy slippers while learning calculus.

In these days of a failing public educational system, some see the Age of Technology as a Great White Hope for students all over the world. In theory, virtual classrooms linking students anywhere on the map to the teachers of their choice seems ideally egalitarian. In practice, however, MOOCs (Massive Open Online Courses) through Udacity, Coursera, and others have garnered mixed reviews. Although hundreds of thousands of students have signed up as of this writing, the attrition rates for dropping out before course completion are sometimes as high as 90%. According to *The Chronicle for Higher Education*, the median number of registrants for MOOC courses that have been offered so far is 33,000. Duke University offered "Think Again" in November 2012 and had the largest enrollment of any Coursera course offered up to that point: 226,652 students. (Imagine a classroom that size.) The course covered how to understand, assess, and construct arguments.

Guess how many students completed the course with a minimum grade to receive a Statement of Accomplishment?

2,274—and this is typical. The average 10% completion rate for all MOOCs seems to indicate that the implementation of new technologies to aid education is still in its infancy. Many educators speculate that the lack of face time with an actual teacher is the culprit in this case, combined with no teacher feedback. Wonder where the Age of Technology will bring our grandchildren's generation?

I for one hope that robo-teachers never replace the warm, engaging educators who know students by name and personally interact with them. MOOCs and other anonymous modalities miss the heart and soul of education.

Bonus:

TEENAGE BRAIN DEVELOPMENT

Jacinth Tracey, PhD

A note about the contributing author: Jacinth Tracey, PhD, is a best-selling author and internationally recognized speaker. For over 25 years she's specialized in helping people achieve the mindset for personal and professional success. Her Wired2Succeed practice is located in Toronto, Canada.

Have you ever wondered why your teenager acts the way they do? Well, to put it bluntly, blame their brain development.

All humans have a brain that continues to develop from about three weeks after conception into early adulthood. It takes almost 30 years for a human brain to become fully mature. By the time we're born, we have all the brain cells that we'll ever have (over 100 billion neurons). It's just that our entire brain isn't mature until later in life. During the first 3 weeks after conception, all humans begin to develop a brain and nervous system. By the time we're born until about age 3, our brain is primed to focus on just a few things that we immediately need for our survival. Specifically, during infancy three areas of our brain (the amygdala, hippocampus and reticular formation) are active, while the rest of our brain remains "offline." That's because nature has made it an infant's main job to focus on storing memories, acquiring language skills and motor development, and increasing their attention span so that they can learn.

By age 14, the brain has greatly increased its ability for intellectual and social skills development. The parietal and temporal lobes have begun to mature. Poorly thought out decisions are common, though, because while their brain has matured considerably since they were born, the main part responsible for logical thinking, planning, and higher-order reasoning (the prefrontal cortex) is still far from mature. The prefrontal cortex is the brain's remote control; it controls impulses, emotions and empathy, and communicates with other parts of the brain by a complex neural network. In general, the prefrontal cortex is what will eventually make your tween or teen an even more pleasant person to be around.

However, you're going to have to wait, because the prefrontal cortex is still developing (it's still immature) and your teen's limbic system is in flux. The limbic system is our "emotional brain." Although it helps with basic health functions like regulating heart rate and blood sugar levels, it also informs things like passion and memories. Part of this system, the amygdala, collects and connects information from the five senses and links them to emotional responses. Its development, along with hormonal changes, may give rise to newly intense experiences of aggression, rage, excitement, fear, and sexual attraction during the teen years.

Because their brains rely more on the limbic system than the more rational prefrontal cortex, teenagers are frequently ruled by feelings more than logic. They are generally still a slave to their emotions, which makes them predisposed to poor impulse control and faulty judgment. This stage of intellectual and emotional development not only baffles many moms and dads, for newcomers to the game of parenting tweens or teenagers it can feel like a total bait and switch. Those adorable kids who used to dance in our kitchens suddenly grow into somber, irrational, or even dangerous teens.

At this stage, teens possess a simultaneous need for both increasing independence and careful oversight. That can create a lot of friction. Many parents don't fully comprehend that the changes in those formerly childlike bodies toward curves and muscle mass is also accompanied by unseen cognitive changes. Although it might make for some tense family dinners, just know that it won't be long until your teenager's brain is fully developed. By the time they are in their late 20s, their brain will finally be intellectually and emotionally mature. It's only at this time that they are primed to make the transition from youth to early adulthood. That's because the prefrontal cortex, the very part of the brain you've been waiting to mature in your teenager, has finally completed its development. Frustratingly, the prefrontal cortex is actually the last part of the brain to mature. At this point, your son/daughter will be more thoughtful, rational and reasonable and be able to consider the consequences of their actions so that they weigh the pros and cons of a situation before taking action. And perhaps the best part, they will be more able to handle and express their emotions in constructive ways.

But for now, you have to deal with the stereotypical teenage brain, with all its intellectual and emotional nuances. For now you have to accept the fact that your teenager will lack judgment and be highly emotional at times. You need to give up on the expectation that your tween or teenager can or will think the same mature way that you do, regardless of how academically proficient they are or what grades they bring home. The infrastructure of their brain is simply not constructed yet; it's still under development.

So how do you get your teenager's brain ready for college, given that it's not yet intellectually or emotionally mature? Well, so far you've done what you need to do. You've passed on your good genetic heritage (genes account for about half of a person's intelligence) and you've provided the best opportunities for intellectual stimulation, emotional resiliency, and learning (social and physical environmental factors, like a safe and nurturing family environment, account for the other half). This is generally referred to as the effects of "nature" and "nurture."

For the most part, the genetic heritage that you've passed on to your teenager is already established. Nature has done all it can to do create the best brain for your teenager. But the story doesn't end there, and that's a good thing. You should know that environmental factors such as diet, social networks, culture, and even stress levels can modify the effect of genes on intelligence (both emotional and intellectual intelligence). That means that you need to make sure that the physical and social environment that your teenager is in supports and enhances their good genetic heritage. What you can do now is to ensure that you maximize that genetic potential, to make sure that their genetic predispositions are working in their favor. As such, even in the teen years, you can indeed continue to influence brain development and continue to wire your teenager's brain for future success. Here are a few things that you can do to help optimize their brain development:

1. Keep an eye on their social influences.

By high school age, your teenager is desperately trying to emotionally separate from the family and form an individual identity. Friends become a particularly valuable social influence at this stage of development. Peer approval becomes so important that if twenty minutes pass without someone commenting favorably on a Facebook status, some teens become emotionally activated. Interestingly, their comments often take a sarcastic tone, as in, "I hate you. Why are you so pretty/perfect?"

Unfortunately, peer influence can take a particularly negative turn at this stage. Eating disorders, agoraphobia, sexual permissiveness, and all sorts of dysfunctional adaptations to this influx of thought ensue. The odd combination of relative isolation as they interact virtually on Tumblr and other social media sites juxtaposed with the universal ability to access the comments and images being flung about have resulted in more than a little tragedy. Cyber-bullying is one problem most parents today can't imagine because our generation didn't live through it.

To complicate things further, research shows that when teens are in groups together, their judgment drops almost proportional to the size of the group. There is data to support the argument that large groups of teens should not be in cars, for example. Perhaps this explains why so many tragically die on graduation night coast to coast. On the plus side, though, it is within these very groups that life skills develop: everything from how to compromise, how to read a room, and how to negotiate to get what they want.

However, as much as you need to monitor your tween's or teenager's social influence (actual and virtual by way of friends and social media) you also need to monitor and regulate the amount of television your teen watches, or rather, the types of programs they watch. Studies show that a lifetime of media consumption can take a toll on how we think, feel and behave. In fact, excessive television watching has been correlated with problems with paying attention and impulse control even later in life.

Peers, watching certain types of television shows, exposure to social media (including the internet) and even playing certain video games are a very real social influence on your teenager. These influences compete to fill their head (and their brain) with views about what they "should" look like and what they "should" become.

At this time it's also crucial to expose your tween or teenager to as many diverse and enriching experiences as possible. Their brains are literally being cultivated toward either greatness or mediocrity, of living a life by their own design or living a life of default. This is not the time to let negative images impact their self-esteem, because it can have dire consequences for their motivation to succeed. This is the time to expose your teenager to positive, healthy images and experiences.

2. Help them to recognize and control their emotional states.

Teenagers (as well as adults) need to be mindful and aware of how their emotional state impacts their actions. Our emotions are in fact what propel us to act (or to avoid and not act at all). Because our emotional state is so critical for our actions and life outcomes, we need to be aware of what is happening in our internal life. This is what helps to develop our emotional intelligence and emotional resilience. When your teenager develops these faculties, it will go a long way to help them handle the various stresses and anxieties that come their way, as well as stimulate the development of their prefrontal cortex to improve rational decision-making.

Emotional intelligence is particularly helpful when your teens are faced with situations that they find stressful or cause them to feel fear. Rather than letting the things in their social environment or even their own feelings spin out of control, having a conscious awareness of what it is exactly they are thinking and feeling in the present moment forces them to focus on what is happening now, rather than stressing out or being afraid of what might happen in the future. They need to learn to become mindful of their own inner thoughts and feelings and how these emotions influence their actions—and their life outcomes.

Decision making is also impacted by our emotions. When your teen is emotional, it's even more difficult for them to focus and to make good decisions. If your teen is in an emotional state (e.g., fearful, anxious, angry, etc.), then his or her decision-making ability will be impacted in a negative way. Think of it this way: thoughts lead to feelings or emotions, and our emotions lead us to act (or not act) in certain ways. Whenever you teenage is emotional, you should know that the emotional parts of their brain (amygdala and limbic system) are calling the shots and not their pre-frontal cortex. It's hard to reason or have a pleasant or neutral conversation with your teen at this point. The best thing that you can do is to wait until your teen settles down to talk about important things (like their college plans), especially if there's any fear or anxiety surrounding this issue.

3. Help them to reduce stress and anxiety.

Adults aren't the only ones who experience stress. The teenage years are filled with stress. There is the stress that comes from trying to fit in with friends, the stress of getting good grades to get into college, the stress about how their future will unfold, and the stress of becoming an adult. Stress (in the form of anxiety and fear) has a profound impact on your tween's or teenager's ability to perform, not just at school but in life in general.

Visualization is a great way to reduce stress and can be used to even reduce the anxiety that comes with taking tests. One of the wonderful things about the human brain is that it makes no distinction between what is real and what is imagined. Therefore, when your teen imagines taking a test and doing well (rather than fearing failing and not getting into college), certain cells in the brain become activated and behave just as they would if they were actually succeeding in real life. The feeling of pleasure (the release of endorphins) and the decrease in stress hormones (cortisol and adrenaline) causes the mind, brain and body to relax. In this state, your teen will be even more able to focus and perform well. This is because visualization wakes up the pre-frontal cortex and helps to improve perception and self-control. By developing the habit of creating healthy and positive visualizations, you can help to train your teenager to reduce stress and to create an "expectation" in their brain for success.

4. Help them to identify their key strengths and core values.

At this time in their life, your teenager has so many influences telling them who they "should" be. They have their friends, the media, their teachers, and yes, they have you. All these voices in their head whispering, if not downright stating, that they know best what your teenager's future "should" look like. This is all happening at a critical time in your teenager's life, just when they are busy trying to figure out their own identity. This internal and external pressure to "become" is bound to cause additional stress, fear and anxiety; especially if your teenager is getting conflicting opinions. And to top it off, oftentimes college entrance requirements often ask your teen to write an autobiographical essay, something that tells the world who they are. If they don't know who they are at their core, even this exercise may cause fear and stress.

The best thing that you can do is to help your teenager identify their key strengths and core values, to decide for themselves who they really are at their core rather than trying to meet everyone else's expectations. What kind of person do they think they are now? What kind of person would they like to become? What do they see at their key strengths (what are they good at)? What are their core values (what is important to them)? What can they contribute to make the world a better place? These kinds of questions will help to orient and focus their minds in the right direction.

5. Love them, even when it's difficult.

Parenthood is perhaps the most heroic of social roles. You get to weather the storms of your precious progeny who insist on butting heads and pushing established boundaries. In fact, your teen might be like many others who seem to perceive conflict, rebellion, and outright mutiny as a type of self-expression. Unable to focus on abstract ideas, they struggle to even consider or understand another's point of view.

Repeat after me: "It's just a phase. It cannot last forever." Then breathe, try to smile, and remember yourself at their age. The best thing that you can do for them (and for your own mental health) at this time is to empathize with their underdeveloped reasoning and their overdeveloped experimentation. Parents have a major role to play here, and it's not always an easy one. We are not here to be their friends. We cannot risk being popular at the expense of doing our job. We are the keepers of the final gate into adulthood—we owe it to them to use our full stable adult brain to help them by staying calm, listening, and being good role models. Part of this requires transparency about our own lives at their age.

Although your son or daughter may sometimes drive you up the nearest wall, the changes in the teen brain provide magical entry into the world that lies ahead. They are assessing the world beyond the horizons of their home, town, state and even country. When you have done your job correctly, they will be both emotionally and intellectually equipped to handle all the challenges that lie ahead and become a positive contribution to the world.

Checklist #1

FOR COGNITIVE INDEPENDENCE

- 🔒 Develop the habit of asking your teen why something is important, or how it works. Work on those deeper reasoning skills daily.
- 🔒 Build their self-advocacy skills by helping them express dissenting opinions and disagreements with key adults in an appropriate way.
- 🔒 Plan summer activities 3-6 months in advance. Target opportunities that will competitively position them in the college applications process, while seeking the balance of downtime and recreation.
- 🔒 Initiate a dialogue about the realistic job prospects for their possible career plans. Help them aim for "new millennium" jobs with real needs for qualified candidates.
- 🔒 Assess how they are using—or possibly abusing—technology. Help them find independence from over-usage.
- 🔒 Remember your teen's brain is "under construction"—don't expect an Autobahn before the ramps are all connected.

Key #2

EMOTIONAL
INDEPENDENCE

Chapter 4

MENTORS

We must walk consciously only part way toward our goal and then leap in the dark to our success.

—Henry David Thoreau

Collège readiness requires more than cognitive preparation. Emotional independence is the second key students need. I have often said that detours dictate destinations, and those detours are often related to emotions. Mentors guiding teens to the right goals are often MVPs for parents who've recognized they have to begin to emotionally let go.

You've probably heard the colloquialism "time to loosen the apron strings." The image of a grown adult still tied to a parent's control or dominance is rarely a good thing. Capable individuals mustn't remain dependent or they will stunt their emotional growth.

The family dynamic when older teens remain tied to apron strings damages both them and their parents. Apron strings aren't made of elastic—they are not intended to stretch and pull. They are made to tie and then release. Fathers and mothers, daughters and sons—all must make peace with the necessary steps toward the teen's eventual individuation.

Think of this process as akin to having a phantom limb. Just as 60-80% of amputees have the sensation that an amputated or missing limb is still attached to the body, many parents experience a similar sense of confusion and loss as they try to emotionally release their teen, that once-bouncing baby who has been so attached to them for all these years.

Here are some strategies to help you as a parent with that phantom limb feeling. Just remember, part of launching your teen for college is learning to let go. Yes, it hurts, but you must do it. In the end, you are not losing a child. You are gaining a fully functional adult.

Your Role in Their Hero's Journey

A teen cannot be the hero in their own journey as long as they are an appendage or extension of mom and dad. Joseph Campbell presented the idea of embarking on the journey of individuation in his renowned book *The Hero with a Thousand Faces*. This insightful author theorized, in 1949, that key myths from around the world share a fundamental structure. Parents today who read and apply his "monomythic structure" to their teens' lives can find important cues to helping them succeed.

In a nutshell, Campbell describes a number of stages or steps along this journey. I've applied these to our purposes here:

1. Teen starts out in the ordinary world, attached to mom and dad.

2. Teen receives a call to adventure—adolescence! He or she now must enter an unusual world of strange powers and potential events (Procreation! Graduation! Lots of other "-ations!")

3. By accepting the call to enter this strange world, the teen becomes a hero who now must face a series of tasks and trials (Peers! Dating! Final Exams!)

4. Heroes find that some trials must be faced alone, but many find assistance with outside mentors. (See next section on this, and note that the parent is never, by definition as the point of origin for the journey, the mentor.)

5. At its most intense, the hero-teen must survive a severe challenge, often with help earned along the journey.

6. As the less mature child-teen endures on the road of trials, they may achieve a great gift, "the boon," signifying a threshold of new self-knowledge.

7. The mature hero-teen must then decide whether to return with this boon to the ordinary world (i.e., move home with mom and dad, possibly to face entanglement and enmeshment) *or* to use this gift as they move outward into the new world of adulthood to share the "elixir" of all they've learned along the way with mankind.

The world of literature is filled with examples of young adults coming of age. Your teen has probably read many texts from this category. From *Romeo and Juliet* to *The Outsiders*—individuation is the name of the game and the central conflict of the narrative. Interestingly, the discord these young people face frequently flows from questionable life choices their parents have made. From Lord

Capulet telling Juliet to "Hang, beg, starve, die in the streets" if she will not marry his choice of husband for her, to the aching absence of parents in the lives of Ponyboy and Sodapop, parental legacy massively influences adolescent outcomes.

What might we be leaving our kids to "clean up?" Lord Capulet left little room for Juliet's future agency in his stubbornness to reign supreme. Whether addiction, violence, crime, or other societal dynamics robbed the *Outsiders* gang of a healthy family of origin, few would argue that the novel would carry such bittersweet longing if conscious parents had been in place for every character. Problem is, parents can't launch teens successfully when our own unfinished business and obstacles deter that process.

Some parents cast a long shadow—are you one of them? I've noticed two types of shadows cast that particularly challenge teens. The first consists of high-achieving parents. Look at the elite families of New York or Europe to see what privilege and easy access to money has wrought in many lives. From addiction to jail, it seems likelier for a camel to pass through the eye of a needle than for a trust-fund baby to find its own way in life. High achieving parents tend to lead too much. I've known parents with Ivy League pedigrees whose teens were quietly traumatized by the thought of not making the cut into the family Alma Mater.

A second category is comprised of disengaged parents who tend to be self-absorbed—whether from alcohol, work, drugs, gambling, or some other distraction—and leave behind a legacy of fear and non-attachment for their teens. Human nature leads children to long for healthy connection to parents. When that gets circumvented, things go haywire.

Here's the deal: this key helps us equip the teen for their journey, not to take that journey with or for them. We can provide instruction, sustenance, and hopefully a positive role model for them to follow, but helping them individuate is a dance in which we have to learn when to lead and when to follow.

In my experience, healthy parents with high-achieving students play the role of sidekick. They are not narcissists bending over the reflected glory of their own DNA and seeing the teen as a mere extension of themselves. They recognize the right to full autonomy that this burgeoning adult has, and step aside ever so deftly as more and more independence is earned and required. Humor often flows between the parent and child. A dad once joked in teacher conferences with me about his own struggles with math when his son was failing pre-calc, saying, "Guess he gets it from me. I'll be sure to tell him, 'Sorry, Son!'"

In allowing their own human experiences with overcoming obstacles to encourage their kids' process, parents do them a real favor. A mom I consulted with found genuine connection with her daughter once she acknowledged that all the social pressure of high school once distracted her too. I saw that girl recognize this was not a lecture but an empathetic exchange of information. "Here's what happened to me. Here's what I did about it. Here's how it turned out." For many teens, just knowing that their parents (and teachers) aren't positioning themselves high on a pedestal of perfection opens them up to listen more openly. I've noticed that they are actually hungry for as much information as possible about the trial and error experiences of their family members. Anecdotes trump lectures every time. Allowing children to learn from our mistakes is one of the most precious (and vulnerable) gifts parents give.

Find Five Mentors

As we move from younger childhood into the teenage years, it is so challenging for many parents, myself included. I mean, we give birth to these beautiful little babies and we protect them for many years. Then all of a sudden they seemingly want nothing to do with us. Once you've got a 13 or 15 or 17 year old, their lives become much more independent. We are still hopefully having dinners together several nights a week, and some activities together as a family. But, it shifts.

Mentors play a key role in helping teens develop their inner identity. In Homer's The Odyssey, Odysseus lucked out and got Athena—nothing like having the immortal goddess of wisdom from Mount Olympus guiding your important decisions in life, right? In a way, even for mere mortals that's exactly the kind of role that well-placed mentors can provide. The importance of finding a mentor to work with your teenager is crucial—these individuals help them navigate the later middle school and certainly the high school years with a sense of stereo. That is, not only is mom (who may or may not be the most annoying creature on earth at the moment) saying something, but similar views and values are reflected in the perspectives of others.

Whether it's a tutor or someone in your church, synagogue, or temple, a neighbor or another family member, there is just one rule: it can't be you. Isn't that painful? Don't you wish it could be? I mean, weren't we the ones with the googley eyes and the will to procreate? We gave birth to them. Doesn't it seem like we should be able to be the sun, moon and stars for these children? Um, yeah. Sorry, but the answer is a resounding no.

The goal is to pick five—and here's the catch—try to vary them across as many generations as possible. You may end up with only three, and that's okay, but they should not all be your best friends and of similar age and life experience. Here's a layout of what could work:

1. 20-something sports coach
2. 30-something music teacher
3. 40-something church/temple/synagogue youth counselor
4. 50-something scout leader, family friend, or neighbor
5. Grandparents!

The multi-generational approach allows them to see life from a panoramic view—a full timeline, if you will. This idea actually came to me with a creative writing assignment I was given years ago. The challenge was to write three consecutive short stories about our lives at that point in time from the vantage point of ourselves at three different ages—+10, +20, and +30 years. I was astounded at how differently I was able to see my current challenges through each of those lenses. No doubt, each passage of time brings with it unique gifts and wisdom. Letting teens benefit from as many as possible makes great sense.

We're not here to be their best friends. We cannot be their teachers, their counselors and their only role models. To be a parent is a very high calling, as you know, and if we do the mom or dad thing right, we will be too busy to also be that mentor. After all, part of being an effective parent is living one's own life fully, and bringing one's own dreams to full fruition. They are watching our example, and if we send the message that being a parent has killed our own inner purpose beyond parenthood, that can send a pretty tragic message. No kid wants to feel like they killed mom's chances of becoming an artist, a business owner, or a scientist.

We can help them and we can share with them but we have to sometimes take our hands off the steering wheel and allow other trusted adults to come alongside. Granted, that can be a little frightening, but it's necessary.

Consider who in your circle can offer such support. Of course, this is not necessarily an official thing where you go to your 14-year-old and say, "Hey Johnny, guess what? Here is your mentor!" (I mean, unless you want to see them roll their eyes.) It needs to be subtler in the way that you introduce this relationship to your child's life, but they need a place to go to talk about academic issues and concerns, as well as personal things that come up.

Over my years as an educator, as often as I have been asked to help with things that have to do with academic projects and homework assignments and test prep, probably 20% of the time students are reaching out asking about help with a personal situation—with their boyfriend or girlfriend, for example. Or "Something happened last week at school and I feel kind of weird about it, can we spend the last five minutes of session talking about that?" This is a sacred privilege that a parent entrusts. Certainly if anything major comes up, I always communicate with the parents. Hopefully your mentors would do the same.

Teens need to feel they have multiple sounding boards. One example of a time I had to approach the mom was when the daughter confided in me that she had been self-injuring— her rolled-up sleeve told the story of a teen in severe emotional distress over the parents' divorce. I was touched that she trusted me, and let her know that this was not a situation in which I had the option of maintaining silence. She actually seemed relieved that I would intermediate as her voice with her mother. The girl got help, and last I heard she was stabilized, graduated, and living a normal life. Oftentimes, it's not about doing anything, or even about the advice. It's about actively listening and affirming.

I can tell you from experience—when my firstborn was in high school it was really challenging for me. Her individuating made me insecure. As a first timer on the parent-of-a-teen merry-go-round I thought, "Hey, what am I? Chopped liver?" But what she was actually doing was creating a circle of other voices that she could trust, which would help her navigate. Indeed by the time she got to college with her degree in psychology and graduated, I was just astounded at what she had created for herself. This wasn't because I was the one holding her hand the whole way, but because—even though it was painful—I had to let go and trust some of these other people to help.

At least two or three mentors who are not their parents and not relatives need to be in the lives of students to begin helping them build a vision for who they are in the world separate from the parent.

As they say, it takes a village. So let the village help.

Apprenticeships and Internships

Learning happens in the classroom of life, not at our parents' feet. By the time teens are in high school, an excellent way to promote emotional independence is through finding them a place to shine. This begins with noticing what they're good at doing. What comes naturally? Who in your community is doing that professionally? Many parents underestimate the willingness of other adults to encourage young people with opportunities. Throughout history, apprenticeships have been a primary way young adolescents transitioned to adulthood, and today need not be any different. Whether it's volunteering for a weekend event or participating in a formal internship, the self-esteem that comes to teens when they are allowed to contribute to an actual work endeavor is substantial.

I've seen a boy interested in economics working part time for a local bank and building his resume by the age of fifteen. I've known a girl fascinated by cosmetology already working the shampoo bowl and making connections at a top salon in her neighborhood in her junior year of high school. Notice that these were not jobs someone posted an ad for, but opportunities created by the students themselves at the encouragement of some savvy parents and mentors. Sometimes you have to be willing to stick your foot in the door instead of waiting to be asked. Squeaky wheels get grease, and proactive teens move ahead more quickly than their passive peers.

- Get online with your teen and begin a neighborhood search for businesses specializing in a field they think they might be interested in pursuing.
- Help them create a polished letter of introduction explaining who they are, their passion for the field, and that they will happily work for free for a period of time (2 to 3 months is pretty standard).
- Resist the urge to include anything at all about mom or dad in the letter. This is a red flag for business owners, especially for teens under 16. They need to show their independent motivation and navigate any negotiations solo.
- In exchange for the experience, instead of pay, recommend that they simply seek an eventual letter of recommendation. One great letter from a bona fide business owner in the community can launch them to higher pay positions at the entry level when the time comes. Start humble; end lucrative.
- Enclose at least 1 to 2 letters of recommendation (important: not phone numbers, but pre-written glowing

letters from teachers, mentors, etc.—letterhead stationary is great if they have it).

- Consider enclosing a smiling, well-lit photo.

Inspired apprenticeships and internships help college applications stand out, because they constitute both job skills and the inherent relationship skills needed to sustain them. In some way, the conversation is often personal: one human being connects to another in a profound way. This is decidedly not just a robotic exercise of dispensing information—like one of those machines with a gypsy head in a glass box at a theme park, where you plug in your quarter and it spits out a piece of paper with some random, disconnected prediction of fame and glory. Apprentices learn by doing, and those who oversee them are not Pez dispensers, but guiding forces in the real day-to-day demands of a chosen field of work.

Apprenticeships help students develop an important but invisible "X-factor" in their interpersonal communications, namely emotional intelligence. According to *Psychology Today* magazine, emotional intelligence is the ability to identify and manage one's own emotions and the emotions of others. It describes a sort of emotional awareness that really successful adults possess. How can we ensure our teens get that skill set?

- By securing opportunities for them in summertime, starting no later than 8th or 9th grade, to work cooperatively with others—perhaps in a camp, at an office, or with a community service agency.
- Demonstrating our own effectiveness as emotionally intelligent adults, while underscoring similar traits in other mentors and adults in their lives.

- Positively reinforcing them when they mature in this important area—for example, praising their commitment to working through a challenging group dynamic in a group project with sensitivity to both the participants and the desired outcome.

Notice that through apprenticeships, teens get a taste for actual responsibility. Unlike school, where they participate as members of a group, on-the-job training allows them to function as solopreneurs, and to see real life application of skills they are already learning in the more sterile confines of a classroom.

What could be more fascinating for a teenager interested in mock trials than assisting behind the scenes at a law office? Imagine your fourteen year old volunteering weekends to help a professional animal care specialist at the local pet shelter, while building a resume and portfolio of experiences to move them along their way to becoming a veterinarian. These are potentially pivot points for young adults—but they don't come without some guidance.

As a corollary, if you or someone you are close to owns a business and can provide such opportunities, by all means "get it out there" to a local high school guidance department and pay it forward to deserving young people with the kinds of real-life application experiences that money can't buy and college can't teach.

Reminder: be sure your teen cleans up his or her Facebook, Instagram, Twitter, Pinterest and other social media before sending out queries. Nowadays, the first thing many potential employers do is look at public profiles. The presentation should be congruent with who they are presenting themselves to be in that letter of introduction. In a pinch, some teens have actually created pseudonyms for those accounts and post their off-color humor under a nickname. Just ensure their legal name stays pristine. They will need it.

Chapter 5

GOALS

Cat: Where are you going?
Alice: Which way should I go?
Cat: That depends on where you are going.
Alice: I don't know.
Cat: Then it doesn't matter which way you go.
　　　　　　　　—Lewis Carroll, *Alice in Wonderland*

Lewis Carroll's charming tale of a girl trying to come of age highlights the paradox of adolescence. No matter which way we turn, sometimes the journey can feel nonsensical and circuitous at best. The physics of the classic game of Mousetrap are similar—rolling a single marble through a maze to produce an entertaining and random series of events. Two of my favorite movies, *Chitty Chitty Bang Bang* and *Pee Wee's Big*

Adventure, showcase charming sequences in which the inventors customizing shortcuts to make breakfast delights the moviegoer.

For teens, the notion of cause and effect may not be as concrete as a plate of sausage and eggs cooking over an open flame, à la Dick Van Dyke. Parents need to help them see the connections between what they do and how life responds. Getting them ready for college admissions success requires a series of maneuvers, with many mini-goals along the way. Let's look at a few strategies to help position the right mindset.

Help Them Set Goals That Matter

Your teen lives in a country whose democracy is rooted in the principles of capitalism and the golden rule (often referred to facetiously as "he who has the gold makes the rules"). By definition, the sorts of messages that permeate the media they consume—from popular music to films and television programming—makes several wrongheaded assumptions about the goals of education, and by extension, life.

- That money buys happiness
- That success means financial affluence
- That goals must be tangible rather than intentional

Teens need to have some sense of where they're going, and tethering that destination to something real is a good idea or good intentions can disappear faster than the Cheshire Cat. A perfect example: we all need a certain amount of money in order to enjoy life. But money is a thin veneer of a goal, whose substance is hiding a world of something else beneath. So, now is as good a time as any to ask them five key questions to clarify where they're heading:

1. **What is your overall purpose in this life?** Many teens will stare blankly at this. Let them. Just allow the rhetorical question to settle and simmer in silence. It will loosen them up for the following ones.

2. **What goals would you like to accomplish within the next 10 years?** For this one I recommend a brainstorm together, maybe on a big piece of blank paper with colored markers and icons/art. Don't settle for "to be happy"—that's a cop-out. Also try to avoid making this list digitally. Now is not the time for Google docs. Move color across a page, physically. Ask them: "Happy how? How does that happiness look, feel, sound, taste?" Challenge them to be specific.

3. **What goals would you like to accomplish within the next 5 years?** Have them "chunk it down"—what has to happen within the next 5 years to get to that 10-year goal?

4. **What goals would you like to accomplish within the next 2 years?** Again, simplify it—what movement do they need to generate now to set themselves up for the 5 (and eventually, 10) year goals?

5. **What do you hope to accomplish between now and 6 months from now to help you get there?** Have them make a list of 3 to 5 mileposts along the way for each time frame.

By encouraging your teen to think big picture and incrementally along the way from today until that vanishing horizon line called "the future," you will help them target tangible goals that will prepare them for success on their own terms.

Here are a few favorite goals I've seen among my students over the years. I share them here to give you an idea of what works nicely to position teens for attainable goals:

- to serve mothers and infants in need through my work as a NICU nurse
- to create a stable family environment with my eventual partner and adopt at least one child with special needs to make a positive difference in the world
- to travel internationally sharing my passion for art and music
- to build a non-profit business dedicated to raising public awareness about bullying

Notice that each of these young people had an "other" in mind as they set their goals. Although some teens will begin with inflated talk of Ferraris and mansions, when you scratch the surface what they are really hoping to create is a sense of security and, yes, of purpose. Helping them decipher for themselves what they can *give* before they get all tangled up in what they might *get* will often pull them from empty material things to the relationships that generally lead to actual joy in life. And hey, if they can drive those adopted kids home to their mansion in that Ferrari, more power to them.

Show Them How to Break the Blame Cycle

One of the most common dynamics I see between teens and their parents is a cycle of blame. If the teenager has a D in Chemistry, they frequently blame the "boring teacher," the "loud students in the class," and sometimes even the parents for "not helping me with my homework." The reality may be absolutely accurate that the teen is facing each of those dynamics, but by high school they must become personally accountable for the cause and effect of choices that they themselves are making.

When teens focus on excuses, parents need to help shift that bad habit into a new default mode in which they look for what they can do to change things for the better. Cause and effect, like the truism that we all reap what we sow, must be experienced firsthand to foster the emotional independence teens need to launch successfully. It is unlikely, if not virtually impossible, that a teen who has never been held accountable for their own actions will magically go to college and begin making better choices.

Two extreme tendencies to avoid: a sense of entitlement ("I'm special, therefore the usual rules don't apply to me") and a sense of despair ("Nothing I do will really matter anyway, so why put forth all the extra effort to bring about a result I say I want?").

Of course, some excuses for poor choices are valid, but many excuses are simply that: thoughts immature teenagers use to excuse themselves from living up to their responsibilities. This can range from mistaken choices in personal issues like chores and family obligations (prioritizing a friend's last-minute keg party over Grandma's birthday event) to educational and career matters (feigning being sick at school to play hooky with a friend, and failing an assignment or test as a result). When confronted by parents, often these teens want to shift the focus away from their responsibility and exercise impressive creativity as they mentally justify why this failed grade or hurt grandparent is not actually their responsibility.

Joseph Campbell once wrote, "Your life is the fruit of your own doing. You have no one to blame but yourself." As difficult as it can feel to do so, parents must sometimes shift the teen's gears like an old Camaro—*back* from excuses and into the reality of the matters at hand: the cause and effect of their choices, and the pattern of personal responsibility that must precede everything they do. Once they leave home, if they are to thrive as emotionally independent beings they will need to have this pattern interruption internalized, and the only way that happens is by someone (usually Mom or Dad) "calling them on their crap"—in this case, their bad habit of shirking.

So it's not simply a matter of "Why didn't you do your homework?" It's about overtly pointing out that the teen had a responsibility, failed to meet it, and created an outcome that wasn't desired. When a teen says, "Failing that test was no big deal, I can still pass the semester with a C," he or she is really saying, "It's not important that I meet my responsibilities."

Likely they will fall into the blame game when they feel guilty, because after all they are good kids at heart, just distracted as they try to find their way. A common fallback might be, "And anyway, it's not my fault since the teacher is so _____ (pick an insulting adjective: boring, lame, stupid, annoying, etc.)." Consider responding to this diversionary tactic by saying, "We're not talking about whose fault it is that you didn't want to study. We're talking about whose responsibility it was to do the studying and actually pass that test. And that responsibility was yours."

Shifting the focus back onto the teen's responsibility is actually empowering for them. Although the bad habit of blaming others can be harder to stop than coffee and cigarettes, teens learn to stop trying to pass the buck when mom and dad know how to recognize the tactic for what it is: smoke and mirrors. By avoiding getting stuck in an argument about the nature of the excuse, which easily happens if we're not aware, parents redirect the moment as an opportunity to teach one of the most crucial lessons of adulthood: doing the right thing, not just the easy thing.

Without the parent's consistent guidance in this area, the teen learns to make better and better excuses for poor choices and misbehavior, not to grow up and become emotionally competent. Think of it this way—avoid getting mired down in particulars of the misbehavior, and focus instead on the bigger issue: assuming personal responsibility.

Three years from now, it may not matter that they skipped that review period for the midterm exam, but if the pattern of shirking responsibility becomes entrenched you could have a bigger problem on your hands, like how to get this grown kid out of your house, where they play Xbox all day and expect you to do their laundry. Parents can pay now or pay later. Teach them to be proactive rather than reactive, and lead by example—or get ready to have a permanent boarder.

Help Teens Find Their True North

> *There is a time in every man's education when he arrives at the conviction that envy is ignorance; that imitation is suicide; that he must take himself for better for worse as his portion; that though the wide universe is full of good, no kernel of nourishing corn can come to him but through his toil bestowed on that plot of ground which is given to him to till.*
>
> —Ralph Waldo Emerson, *Self-Reliance*

A particular star that has always fascinated me is Polaris, which is commonly called the guiding star and points the way to astronomical "north" within one degree. All teens can benefit from a guiding star, and so can we as parents. Polaris is the brightest star in the little bear, or Ursa Minor, and is also thought of as the last star at the end of the panhandle of the little dipper. We know that the three wise men found their way to baby Jesus by following a star. What can we help our teens find by looking up?

Imagine we wanted to travel to the North Pole. Would our compass needle swing northward and plot a path? Nope, finding our life's true north is not that easy. To get to the North Pole, or to true north, just following a compass needle won't work. The Earth's magnetism isn't perfectly aligned with the geographical poles. The difference between true north on a map and the north indicated by an individual's compass can vary significantly. Scientists call that difference the magnetic declination, measuring the angles between true north and magnetic north when plotted on a map. Where this gets really interesting is in the magnetic declinations varying from place to place, depending on the intensity of particular magnetic fields.

Each teen has a different purpose, or magnetism. If one holds out a compass in New Zealand, magnetic north will register at 20 degrees east of true north, but if another holds their compass in Los Angeles, the declination is 12 degrees. The trick is to keep your teen from being swayed by the compelling pull of magnetic north, a point in the arctic regions continually shifting location based on the activity of the planet's magnetic fields. Fluid iron is the cause here—oh yeah, fluid iron in the planet's core acts like a huge bar magnet. (You cannot make this stuff up.)

In the life of a teenager, many things pull and tug them away from their true aim and purpose in life. In fact, it's safe to assume many adults spend large portions of our lives the same way. What can a parent do about it? For starters, remind teenagers that it's always the calling of each individual to find their own true north, without being manipulated by magnetic distractions.

College, ideally, is a vehicle for finding and defining that aim. School should provide a venue to explore what the world has in it, what's been accomplished so far, and the theories and the experiences of other people. But in the end, each person can only experience being himself or herself. Your teen is one of a kind—the only one that will ever be on this planet. Help them maximize more than just their GPA. They need a true enthusiasm for learning to thrive in college.

The things we care about are the things we will invest ourselves in, and without that level of personal care and commitment it is unlikely that either our teens or we are going to really want to participate in the rather excruciating process of self-determination.

Most adults I know would agree that experience has shown them their sense of true north often changes over the course of time, but that they still have always had a sense of personal calling to specific experiences in this lifetime. How many times as a teen did you think a breakup with a boyfriend or girlfriend was devastating, but in retrospect you see it was for the best? So, the window dressing of our lives may change and evolve, but the "plot of ground which is given to us to till" doesn't really change much.

Here are some ways your teen can set their inner compass:

- Identify values that they believe will mean something to them permanently.
- State what they would do as a career for free if they knew they couldn't fail.
- Name one person they most admire, and list the traits that this person possesses that warrant admiration.

- Clarify what has always fascinated them since early childhood, and to examine why.

Remember that life itself is a great classroom, with a syllabus largely determined by what each one of us sets out to accomplish while we're here. Remind them that they're being prepared for something wonderful, so they need to pay attention and set sail mindfully and with full intention.

Chapter 6

STABILITY

Adolescence represents an inner emotional upheaval, a struggle between the eternal human wish to cling to the past and the equally powerful wish to get on with the future.

—Psychoanalyst and author Louise J. Kaplan

Parents can stabilize teens' emotions by helping their sons and daughters navigate the most common challenges that can undermine a sense of emotional balance: shyness, anxiety, and depression. I've observed from my years in the classroom that well over 50% of the graduating seniors I've taught struggled to some degree with one or more of the topics covered in this chapter. College admissions success was correlated with the level of emotional stability.

Getting through adolescence is no picnic. From acne to grades to peer pressure, it can feel like one big smorgasbord of "get me out of here." In my experience, though, a funny thing happens around January of the senior year of high school—many teens suddenly long for the relative safety and predictability that being tethered to a schedule brought. If you're like me, you want to help them successfully plot a course through some common emotional minefields.

Sometimes we can begin by encouraging our teens to "count their blessings." As trite as this idea is, there is much to be said for awareness of what is good in life, not just lamenting what "sucks" (to use a much-too-common word). I like to ask them how they are, and then listen carefully to the patterns. I used to have a tutoring client who began every session by answering my "How's it going?" with a long sigh and the same two words, "I'm tired!"

Clearly she was unaware of this pattern, so one day I plainly asked her why. She seemed startled. Once we spoke more, I realized that she was under a tremendous amount of pressure to perform at a high academic level, and the "tired" was not physical, it was emotional. By opening up a dialogue next time I was with both her mother and her, we were able to get to the root of a need she had—namely, a moratorium on perfectionism and some latitude to make mistakes.

I also recall a male student who punctuated the mid-session break in our two-hour AP tutoring sessions with an extended trip to the bathroom. When he'd come back, his red eyes and hemp-ish aroma belied an addiction that neither he nor his mother wanted to acknowledge. This made it virtually impossible for me to do my job, which was to help him memorize literally hundreds of facts, and synthesize them into cogent essays. It's kind of hard for them to be profound when they've got the munchies and just want to watch Cheech and Chong movies.

Teens like this can't tell us how they "are," because they don't know. Or maybe they do, but they've submerged their anger, fear or depression beneath layers of survival behavior. I knew one 15-year-old who was so obsessed with makeup that she would not leave her home without 1 to 2 hours of primping—every hair in place, and a full face of foundation, blush, eyeliner, and lipstick—just to go to school on a rainy Tuesday. She fell behind in her studies because of a desire to maximize her outsides, even while her insides lost focus. Her parents had to help her find her way out of overcompensation and into self-acceptance.

In extreme cases, I have worked with students over the years who literally self-injure or even attempt suicide. There can be no doubt that the emotional pain preceding such actions must have brewed whether undetected or not for many months if not years. Yet kids cut their thighs, scrape their arms raw, pull their hair and eyebrows out, and enter into eating behaviors that can easily lapse into anorexia and bulimia. What can a parent do?

Teen Emotional Challenge #1: Anxiety

Occasional stress accompanies modern life, but when it veers out of control for teens it can get in the way of their schoolwork, physical health, and emotions. I have known young teens with diagnosed anxiety disorders where conflicts in school resulted in full-blown panic attacks. For those who have an anxiety disorder, seek treatment from a health professional. Here are some pieces of advice I've seen help teens manage anxiety:

- **Commit to getting enough sleep—at least 7 to 8 hours.** Many teens are natural night owls, but with

6:30 a.m. alarms, they should not be up past 10:30 p.m. on school nights.

- **Cut out eating late at night, especially sugary drinks with caffeine.** I've seen anxiety worsen in kids with poor eating habits like frequent fast food and few veggies. Junk in, junk out.

- **Try to get some kind of physical activity in for 30 minutes every day.** Handling the roller coaster of life is a lot easier with exercise sending oxygen to every cell in their bodies—this helps brains and bodies thrive.

- **Allow them to "chillax" with friends.** Sometimes teens feel pressure to make everything into an organized activity. Be sure they know they can simply hang out at your home or with a friend without everything needing to be built around a movie, party, or other event.

- **Breathe!** Staring at a TV or computer screen isn't true relaxation. All those electromagnetic bursts and light disrupt the mind's natural need for peace and quiet. Get outside—walk in a park, toss a Frisbee with a dog. Anxiety fades away in the presence of conscious, deep breathing—like in t'ai chi or yoga. It has an actual physical effect on the mind, relaxing the nervous system and sending a message to the entire body to loosen up.

- **Avoid alcohol, drugs, and tobacco.** Don't delude yourself—if they haven't tried them, they are surrounded by kids who have. Welcome to America. Now: talk to your child. Help them understand the connection between marijuana and paranoia, which is a form of anxiety. Help them to recognize the impact of alcohol on their emotional perceptions, and the role of cigarette tobacco in creating dependency connected to nervousness. Why have them pay for the privilege of making life harder than it has to be?

Teen Emotional Challenge #2: Shyness

My mother tells me I was the shyest of her three children. This surprises me, having evolved into a reasonably extroverted adult. But I can vaguely remember the insecurity that plagued me through mid-adolescence.

I see shyness as an adaptive behavior. Whether at a party or in the classroom, sticking one's neck out there to possible judgment and ridicule can keep the most effervescent teen ducking for cover. Although there's nothing wrong with being introverted, the delineation between introversion and shyness marks the difference between a possibly well-adapted teen and one who flies under the radar because of inhibition or outright fear.

As reported by *Psychology Today* magazine, 50% of Americans taking the Myers-Briggs Type Indicator personality test qualified as introverts. The MBTI defines introversion as a preference for solitude, reflection, and internal exploration of ideas as opposed to active engagement in the external world. If this sounds like your teen, it is important to ensure they are not overwhelmed.

Of course, introversion and extroversion can be thought of on a graduated scale, with normal distribution across the population of all teens. There are a few extremely extroverted students in most schools, and a few extreme introverts, while most fall somewhere in between.

The challenge is helping teens to access and cultivate personal energy in a way that feels authentic. Many so-called "shy" teens actually enjoy social interactions of a certain kind— I've seen quiet kids from class blossom to life when attending Homecoming dances and proms I've chaperoned, for example.

Back in the classroom, though, the quiet nature returned, and that is okay. Teens need to know it's okay not to compare themselves to others. It's too easy for that to lapse into self-doubt and self-flagellation.

Some teens truly need resonance, not stimulation; intimacy not superficiality; depth not merely breadth. The labels, although tempting, can only serve them so far. Help them focus awareness on what behaviors serve their higher goals.

Shyness is potentially more damaging to a teen than mere introversion, though, in that social reticence and discomfort are the hallmarks of shyness. When teens are completely opposed to social activity, they often feel lonely despite the self-imposed isolation.

Try to assess whether your teen is introverted, or truly shy. Does he or she thrive best in quiet environments, interacting one on one? Simply being independent from needing external rewards to be happy can be a positive thing, as long as they feel good about their lives. If they are crippled by self-doubt, however, it might be time to get some counseling.

What Not to Say to a Shy Teen

Shy teens might seem harmless and sweet most of the time, but they can be ignited to quick anger when others don't honor their personal comfort zones. Avoid the following:

- "Don't you like parties? Why don't you want to go?" Shy teens avoid parties, sporting events and dances for many reasons, from self-consciousness about their weight to being utterly convinced they will be ridiculed if they go. Until the inner reason for isolating is addressed, best to steer clear of awkward situations. There may actually be a good reason they are not ready to cross that threshold. Don't push them.

- "I just can't understand why a nice (guy/girl) like you doesn't seem to have many friends." Shy teens know others are more "popular" than they are. Having a parent point it out can rub salt in the wound.

- "Hurry up and answer me. Why do you always take so long to reply?" Be careful not to interrupt them when they finally get talking. They often feel overlooked or unheard. Don't make it worse.

How to Help Your Teen Overcome Shyness

As we've said, a quiet or introverted teen can be perfectly happy, but when social situations are totally rejected, it might be time to offer tips to help them out:

- Help them brainstorm a few ways to start a conversation with someone they'd like to know better. Both on the phone and in person, have them practice phrases like, "Are you going to the game Friday night?" and "Wow, I love that color you wore today." Innocuous but friendly banter can really open new relationships, but shy kids need practice.

- Let them also practice role-playing physical behaviors with you as if you're someone they want to know. Help them understand the importance of a firm handshake or a warm hug, of eye contact, and especially of smiling. Without criticizing, help them see that they can build their confidence. Some shy teens facially grimace, unaware. Sensitive feedback and compassionate support are crucial.

- Help them to understand that being assertive does not mean being aggressive, and that they can positively impact both their academic and social lives by speaking and opening up. It's a lot easier to love a butterfly than a cocoon.

Teen Emotional Challenge #3: Depression

What's the difference between a situationally "bummed" teen and one who is actually depressed? After all, teens ride the hormone roller coaster for years, and feeling sad or blue is par for the course when a friendship has ended or they've failed a test. There is nothing "wrong" with a sad teen. Parental radar needs to engage, however, when a week or two of moping around after a letdown turns toxic.

I've seen teenage girls break down in tears in the middle of English class, only to be giggling at the lunch table two hours later. Teenagers can be remarkably resilient. Just keep an eye out for indicators that sadness is becoming systemic. Dropping grades can be one sign that their ability to focus is being hampered by their emotional distractions. Sharp changes in weight, and physical appearance changes like odd clothing or lack of hygiene might also indicate distress. Here are some practical strategies that help.

- **Exercise.** Have them take a nice walk every day—or dance, jog, skate, swim or bike. Depressed teens may not want to be active. Encourage them to do it anyway (ask a friend to exercise with them to make it more appealing). Moods often equalize as good habits develop. In addition to moving aerobically, yoga is a great boon for evening out moodiness. Have them try child's pose, or simply lie on their back on a carpet with their legs up a wall. Two other aspects of yoga—breathing exercises and meditation—can also help those battling depression to feel better.

- **Creativity as medicine.** No one wants to see a loved one's creativity and sense of fun disappear, but depression can cause that. Most teens have at least one area that allows them to shine creatively, whether it is in music, visual arts, writing, or making short films for YouTube. Encourage them.

- **Connection.** Consider providing them time in nature and with animals. How about horseback riding? Let them play with kittens at a local shelter and then adopt one. Even simply taking them to natural environments with lots of sunshine and inspiring landscapes can soften their view and let hope back in.

- **Nurture them with good nutrition.** It's no secret that depression can affect appetite. Both extremes—undereating and overeating—can cause problems. Not getting proper nourishment can create a vicious cycle, in which the lack of necessary elements for physical and mental health creates larger and more complex problems in a student's life. Fruits and vegetables, healthy protein, and complex carbohydrates in appropriate amounts are key to giving the body and mind what they need to thrive.

- **Someone (or something) to talk to.** Are there any particular life situations that may have contributed to their depression? If you know what's got them feeling blue and why, try to talk about it. Look for non-threatening times like driving or doing another activity to chat. They may just need a sense of understanding, whether from you or a trusted friend. Some teens also benefit from writing in a journal. I had one as a teenager that really helped me process both positive and difficult aspects of my life. A cute notebook and colorful felt markers can be a great little pick me up gift for this purpose.

- **Gratitude lists.** When all of life seems grim, negative, and hopeless, teenagers are in real distress. How can we reach them? Some teenagers may truly need professional help, and when this is the case, run— don't walk—to the nearest counselor. I like the idea of a gratitude list, where every aspect of life for which one is grateful gets catalogued—big (good health) and small (Reese's). By putting "gratitude in the attitude" and counting blessings instead of complaints, many teens (and adults) are able to reframe circumstances and rediscover their equilibrium.

- **A positive mindset.** Experts often assert that optimists live longer than pessimists. While we can't force our kids to be optimistic, we can help them notice patterns of the way they speak about life. If they are entrenched in pessimism, that's no more fun for parents than it is for the teachers who work with them at school. It's important that we help them foster internal dialogue that can then hopefully catch up with their external one. When they say "I'm bored" an effective parent is equipped not with sarcasm or criticism, but with another way of framing that feeling. "You must be ready to find a worthy activity to fill these next few hours before your appointment. What might be some options?" Do not flinch when they say the words "nap" and "Xbox." Just gently and kindly redirect them to their goals.

Double Trouble: Inertia and Impulsivity

Both inertia and impulsivity can erode a teen's ability to become emotionally independent. Inertia, defined here as thinking without acting, presents one extreme. Impulsivity, that goblin of acting without thinking, is equally problematic.

In scientific terms, inertia measures the resistance of the body to changes in motion. If you've ever tried to rouse a sleeping teenager on a weekend morning to take an SAT exam, you know the lethargy that must be overcome to get them vertical, eating scrambled eggs, and out the door for a 7:45 check-in time at the local auditorium. Momentum is mass in motion and is defined as mass times velocity—this equation describes the physics of a typical teen exiting the last class of the school year and heading to the parking lot to meet up with their friends.

In my experience, much of teen inertia originates with a fear of failing and disappointing themselves or their parents. They end up not trying at all in an attempt to appear not to be emotionally invested in the outcome. As frustrating as this inertia can be, here are some strategies to motivate momentum.

- Help them see why this momentum benefits them in the end. Appeal to your teen's desire for independence, and let them know that you are not nagging, but actively preparing them for the independence right around the corner in their future.

- Without being punitive (which generally backfires anyway) reward your teen with privileges they want. It may be computer time, playing video games, cell phone apps, or concert tickets. Note: this doesn't work if you've already created a climate of entitlement, so evaluate whether it might be time to pull back on the spoiling.

- Use structure and predictability to help them see cause and effect. For teens with poor time management skills, placing a deadline or a schedule on expectations will help motivate them to follow through.
- Be sure to reward right choices—catch them doing good things and make it a big deal. One great rule of thumb is to praise at least twice for every one boundary or criticism you mete out. Check your own ratios—you might be surprised how easily it is to fall into the negativity trap.
- Allow your child to feel discomfort and anxiety from the consequences of poor choices. Failure can provide a powerful motivation. It produces a sense of discomfort that can spark a teen to choose differently next time. Avoid allowing a tolerance for mediocrity to develop.

Choices lead to consequences—this is the central message they need to internalize. It can spell disaster when parents try to circumvent this necessary part of parenting. For example, I once had a student who showed no motivation whatsoever to complete a school project due the next day. His mother actually stepped in and completed the assignment for him.

Overly indulgent parents, in spite of their good intentions, perpetuate the cycle of inertia again and again. This echoes in basic chores, too. Some parents get so exhausted trying to get teens to clean their rooms or help vacuum they just do it themselves to avoid the confrontation. Bad idea. Choices lead to consequences in real life—i.e., their future boss will fire them if they simply opt to ignore an assignment—and so they must do the same thing in your home if they are going to be prepared to launch.

Impulsivity is our other "I" culprit—where the willingness to take action is there, but the action taken is poorly thought through. Emotional independence requires careful navigation of two opposite inclinations. As inertia teeters, impulsivity totters as a contradictory but equally damaging tendency.

Science teaches that impulsiveness stems from a brain imbalance between two linked systems—something called the incentive processing system, which anticipates and processes rewards and punishments, and the cognitive control system, which is associated with logical reasoning and impulse regulation.

Emotional maturity is both a matter of the heart and of the mind. The incentive processing part of the teen brain begins changing rapidly with the onset of puberty, causing teenagers to become more responsive to rewards and prone to seeking sensation even when adults can see the fallout long before it occurs to the teen that there might be negative consequences for their actions. This is because the cognitive control piece of teen brain development develops at a much slower rate well into the twenties, and so teens often lack the foresight to guide the impulse control parent hope to see. Their hearts are in the right place, but the brain *no comprende*—the translation doesn't always make sense.

It's basically like the manual transmission on a car—teens can accelerate from zero to ninety, but don't have much of a braking system in place yet. Worse: they often pop the clutch as they shift gears. I can remember learning to drive my mom's navy blue 1969 VW Beetle at age 16, and I couldn't tell you which of us was more erratic—me trying to shift from third to fourth gear on Route 66, or me trying to navigate life's choices as an easily distracted teen in small-town America. I probably stalled that car every week for the first month, as I slowly figured out the nuanced relationship between clutch and accelerator.

Educators have long known that middle adolescence, from ages 14 to 17, presents an especially vulnerable period. The disparity between the two systems is at its largest, so thinking before acting doesn't always occur naturally. The inclination to lurch for immediate gratification rather than delaying rewards can make teens rash in their decisions, often to their own detriment.

If it's true that the waiting is the hardest part of life, then that explains why teens avoid it when they can. In fact, most young adults are well into their 20s before they truly develop the anticipatory skills of cause and effect that lead to both personal and professional success. Watching out for inertia and impulsivity can help them avoid lots of pitfalls on the road to college success.

THE 12 PILLARS
OF PERSONAL POWER

Simon Treselyan

A note about the contributing author: Simon Treselyan is an internationally noted author and motivational speaker. As a former Special Operations agent in the British Special Forces, he draws upon a 19-year military background as he specializes in maximizing human potential.

The Pantheon was a building constructed in order to honor the gods of Ancient Rome. Ancient man created the Pantheon's 12 strong pillars as a massive and support to the roof of the Pantheon, one of the most impressive structures ever created. The 12 pillars represent 12 powerful character traits that promise to generate fulfillment for those who embrace them:

1. Be Authentic

Perhaps this is the greatest challenge and exploration on this planet. By attempting or even hoping to convince someone that they are something other than they truly are, young adults reveal a belief pattern: "What I truly am is not good enough for you and certainly not good enough for me." How disempowering. Teens must be reminded they are already valid, even as they . . .

2. Act As If

"Fake it 'til you make it" is a mindset that creates the mental and emotional environment needed to progress in life. By "acting as if," brain synapses fire in a similar fashion as the authentic behavior. The brain and mind cannot differentiate between what is real and what is imagined. The more teens "act as if," the more what they are looking to create will catch up to them.

3. Pay Attention

As teens learn to pay attention they are essentially making an affirmation that the directing of mental resources, aligned with time, is worth the effort—for they will achieve something from that action. This is perhaps the most basic element of personal growth. Attentive awareness is not a casual state of mind.

4. Speak the Truth

When teens elect to speak the truth as a commitment to their own growth, they actually align themselves with a tremendous internal power. Truth brings a number of complimentary side effects, all of which aid their development and the strength of their relationships with others. Integrity, trust, and respect are all by-products leading to a life with more depth. Bonus: when they tell the truth there is much less to remember.

5. Be Congruent

No one likes a bad photocopy. Teens need to learn to be proud of how they were each uniquely designed in order to develop into who they were meant to eventually become. Being able to honestly gauge and assess their own strengths and weaknesses is one of the real steps to personal power.

6. Be Direct

Knowing what they want is a prerequisite to asking for it, and teens need to be taught how to be specific. This pillar of personal power may almost appear too simple to bring about results. Do not underestimate the power of a teen being able to ask for what they actually want.

7. Take Responsibility

Your teen needs to be reminded that they are responsible for how they choose to react to any event or person. Others are not responsible for how they react or feel. No one can make them happy, sad, or anything at all. Self-mastery requires being in control of internal emotions, being proactive and not merely reactive.

8. Keep Agreements

Being accountable to others is a valuable asset. Reliability and integrity result when people honor agreements. Being known for following through on a promise creates a feeling of certainty with others that has a direct impact on their lives. Opportunities rise and fall in direct proportion to being trustworthy.

9. Walk the Talk

A good example is more powerful than a great sermon. They say that talk is cheap, and it is certainly easier to chitchat than to tread the harder road of doing what one says. In walking the talk, teens become real. Real people attract real friends, real opportunities, and real results.

10. Never Give Up

Determination means unswerving commitment to a previously identified goal or dream. It has everything to do with focus. Too often, teens lose focus and wander off to chase something shiny and new. Simply bring them back to their purpose by having them ask themselves, "Why am I doing this and how will it positively impact my life?" The more powerful the answer, the more they will be willing to endure the inevitable obstacles along the way.

11. Take Action

Yesterday and tomorrow do not actually exist as realities. They are either memories or projections. Teens, although working toward goals, need to anchor their ambitions to the present moment. The more focused energy invested in the now, the more likely they will create an effective future.

12. Leave Footprints

We are here for such a short period of time. Teens need to be taught that they leave footprints of their presence in all words, deeds, actions and creations. What do they hope to one day leave behind for their children and grandchildren?

These simple tools create dramatic results. The 12 pillars create the kind of character that opens doors in many facets of life. Like the Pantheon itself, your teen's character will endure and produce for them a legacy of fine character and integrity.

Checklist #2

FOR EMOTIONAL INDEPENDENCE

🔒 Evaluate your teen's hero's journey—what stage of Joseph Campbell's roadmap have they reached?

🔒 Help your teen identify their "boon"—what is it they hope to contribute to the world through their unique abilities and efforts?

🔒 Help your teen secure five mentors who will play key roles in their transitional lives, ideally one from each age-decade of 20s, 30s, 40s, 50s, and older.

🔒 Look at your own list of work colleagues, friends, and acquaintances and consider which have something to offer your teen in a field of interest to them. Seek apprenticeships starting by 9th or 10th grade if possible.

🔒 Help your teen create a "True North" list, with 10-year, 5-year, 2-year, and shorter timelines "chunked down" to keep things progressing.

🔒 Help your teen differentiate between blame and responsibility.

🔒 Ask your teen to rate himself or herself on the inertia/impulsivity scale, and ask them what they think is an ideal balance. Help find it.

- Have them assess their personal integrity using the 12 pillars.
- Assess whether professional assistance, whether in the form of therapy, yoga, or life coach, might be a worthwhile investment.

Key #3

PHYSICAL INDEPENDENCE

Chapter 7

APPEARANCE

Adolescence is just one big walking pimple.
　　　　　　　　　　　　　　　—Carol Burnett

N
o parent wants their kids to grow up and live life in dirty sweat pants and grungy hair, stumbling through low paying jobs while clinging to home for survival. Although they may go through periods when their living space smells like a post-game Lakers' locker room, we all assume that someday our beautiful babies will join the shampooed, coiffed and zippered society of productive citizens. Getting into college may not be a physical contest, but there are aspects of the process that take place in the bodily world.

Parents get nervous when basic niceties like grooming and organization don't spontaneously materialize. Even basics like these are actually skills that have to be taught and reinforced. Here are some concrete, physical aspects of life that need special attention for parents to ensure their teens fare well once they've left the nest.

The default of some well-intentioned parents is to simply do things for their sons or daughters. I know of one college freshman during her first semester living in a dorm 40 minutes away who had her mom do her laundry since she had no idea how to wash or dry a load for herself. I get it. Moms often find it easier to make a bed than to compel a teen to do it for themselves.

If the real goal were just a clean house, doing everything for them, or hiring a maid, might make sense. But since the goal is to launch an independent human being, the bar is raised much higher.

This is not just a practical matter; it is about creating integrity and character. There are two reasons that this self-care issue is critical to helping teens establish physical independence. One: if they don't pull it together in terms of hygiene and self-presentation they won't get far professionally. Two: their social lives will likely suffer as well.

Grapple with Grooming

Not many parents can remember the last day they actually bathed their child. When infants arrive, they rush out to buy little plastic tubs and Johnson & Johnson products. By the time their sons and daughters are toddling around and bumping into every table ledge in sight, the time has come to begin weaning them toward independence. Certainly by the time they are in preschool, most children bathe themselves, with a little help from Mommy to rinse the extra bubbles off their ears. It's not so easy with a teen. I've noticed that many fall into one of two categories—either overly concerned with or utterly oblivious to hygiene.

If your teenage son or daughter is not naturally picking up social clues that indicate they are being assessed by classmates, teachers, and others in their lives, now might be the time to break it to them gently. Few people like the smell of a stranger's body odor, and no one wants to see teeth that haven't been flossed or brushed since two bags of Red Hot Cheetos ago. Creating an actual schedule for them might be necessary. On the other hand, if you are the parent of a manic primper, who can barely get out the door in the morning due to all the rituals of hair and body adornment, now might be an important time to help them evaluate the proportion of energy being invested.

We all need a good hairbrush and face washing when we awaken, not to mention some dental care, but for some teens the angst of adolescence can manifest as an Oscar-worthy prep session every morning before school. It's exhausting and counterproductive, and can cause negative peer assessment just as much as under-primping.

Wrap the Package

Teenagers, like adults, benefit from knowing how to optimize their personal presentation. For some, a trip to a dermatologist for treatment is in order if they are prone to acne. I'm sure most of us can remember the horror of a red bump or two appearing the day of a big dance or even a random school day. There are many over the counter products to help keep your teen's complexion clear. Loving parents don't pretend it doesn't matter—because they know in the real world kids can be cruel. Even when they're not, social stigmatization can hurt. Get them to the local drug store at the very least, for some topical remedy to help clear their complexions.

My father once told me that if he'd have known he was going to live this long, he'd have taken better care of his teeth. Having full dentures in his 50s was no fun, and preparing our teens for dental health throughout their adult lives needs to have begun when they were children with regular checkups. Does your teen floss? They should. Not only does this decrease the likelihood of cavities (and costs to fill them), but it greatly improves the circulation in the mouth and appearance of front teeth. If you can afford to get them an electronic toothbrush, they do a terrific job of keeping the plaque away. If their teeth are dingy or yellow, many national brands of bleach strips are currently on the market to inexpensively whiten their smile as they ask out that special someone to prom.

Hair makes a major statement to their peers about who they are in the social pecking order. Students in schools who are behind the times in terms of hairstyles or hair accessories can really draw unkind responses.

I once saw a very sweet sixth grade girl mindlessly get out of her mom's car one morning at drop off wearing a My Little Pony headband. I noticed it was conspicuously missing later in the day. No doubt she hadn't gotten the memo that Hot Topic skulls were way cooler that month than retro-kid culture, and plopped that pink and purple vestige of innocence into her backpack or the nearest trashcan.

Is this great? No. I love the idea of kids wearing and doing what they want—but I am advocating for parents to at least spend some modicum of time exploring other kids in their teens' peer group, and trying to help them not stand out like too much of a sore thumb unless they truly embrace the outsider status it can bring.

Teens deserve a fresh haircut every few months. If you can't afford to buy them one, learn to do it yourself. You can get a decent pair of hair scissors for $25 at a beauty supply store. YouTube is full of instructional videos. Or find a local salon with new trainees and let them do it for a reduced rate. Even long hairstyles benefit from a minor trim on the ends to keep them looking polished.

Consider their body type when shopping for clothing—what flatters? Are you perhaps in the habit of buying the wrong size? If your teen is a girl have you had her sized for a bra by a professional at a lingerie shop? Many teenage girls outgrow from a 32A to a 34B practically overnight. Pay attention if their tops aren't fitting properly and get replacements in a timely manner.

Consider their coloring—what shades make them look great and which drain their appearance? The wrong shade of blue can make a big difference. You don't have to be an artist or a fashionista to help your teen make good choices of colors that flatter their appearance. Of note—many teens try to hide behind a wardrobe almost entirely of one color, usually black. While black is fine for a basic color, you don't want them looking like they work for the local morgue, so see if you can't introduce some variety.

Think about how many changes of clothes they need to not have to repeat the same shirt more than once every few weeks. Trust me, you may not care but your teen's peers will notice. "Ew, isn't he the kid who always wears that same Nike shirt?" is not something you want others saying about your precious child. Even if you need to go secondhand, many army surplus, vintage, and Goodwill shops are quite trendy for many teens. We're not talking about handing them your Visa card to ring up hundreds of dollars of retail at the mall, but teens do need a broad enough wardrobe to fit in with the demands of their increasingly complex lives.

You may be asking yourself why this matters in a book about college admissions. The answer is: I've seen too many students marginalized in interviews and at college fairs because no one helped them "package" themselves in a way that would benefit their goals. Let's not kid ourselves, appearances do count—they impact not only how our teens are perceived by college admissions staff but also by their peers, teachers, administrators, friends' parents, and potential bosses. Teens benefit from learning to "wrap the package"—to make the most of themselves physically for maximum impact socially, academically, and financially. Yes, the inside matters most. But a pretty interior with body odor outside and a filthy appearance won't get them very far in terms of independence.

Teach Laundry 101

Does your teen know how to wash, dry, fold, and iron their own clothes? If not, high school is the time to provide this important instruction for them. I know as a parent that it is so tempting to just do it all ourselves, but as we've established elsewhere in this book, creating that sort of entitlement leads to problems down the road. If our kids honestly think they can throw dirty socks on their floors and they magically wash themselves to appear neatly folded in a drawer the next day, we are perpetuating a myth and exploiting ourselves in the process.

Let them sort their own, and maybe even the family's, full loads sometimes. Hot for whites, warm for colors, cold for blacks. What detergent and how much should they use, which setting and how long? What's a fabric softener, and how can heat keep them from having to iron at all? See, this may seem annoyingly obvious for you and me, but teens whose moms have fallen into the habit of doing it all have no idea about any of that. When they get to college, the dorms don't have moms neatly folding their underwear. Let them slowly acclimate to self-responsibility now.

Let's Get Physical

Has your teen developed an exercise regimen that keeps their bodies strong and actively engaged at least 3 to 4 times a week? The harsh reality is that if they haven't found the structure and discipline to do so while enjoying the relative comforts of living at home with mom and dad, it is unlikely they will launch independently and magically begin jogging for fun.

One great way for teens to stay fit is through sports. According to recent statistics, over 60% of American teens play sports. Whether it's school volleyball or a community soccer league, the regular exercise and social opportunities to build lasting friendships is key. If your teen doesn't like team sports, individual sports like golf or tennis will allow them to be a part of a group while performing solo. If you can afford it, let them join a gym.

Food as Fuel

Does your teen know how to prepare healthy, nutritious foods? Be sure they do. Man does not live by Nutella and pizza alone. 'Nuff said.

Chapter 8

FINANCES

Time to Take the Teen Financial Literacy Quiz

Is your teenager money smart? Find out. Ask them:

1. What are the major categories every young adult should know to include in their budget?
2. Define FICA—what is it and how does it impact all Americans' bottom line in their budgets?
3. What range of numbers represents low, medium, and high credit scores?
4. What is the average cost of rent for a decent one-bedroom apartment in your home community?
5. How much money would it cost to feed them for seven days if they had only an empty refrigerator and cabinets to begin?
6. What minimum percentage of income do experts recommend every working person put away into savings or investments?
7. What is the current cost of a 3 year-old used mid-size car, and what would those monthly payments be if spread across a standard 36-month loan?

8. Medical and car insurance are often hidden expenses that teens don't think about—what is the annual premium for both of these (whether paid now by parents or hypothetical)?
9. Tax bracket reality check: how much tax does the IRS charge a $25,000 per year employee? What if they make $38,000/year? $100,000/year?
10. Define bankruptcy and its legal rules.

Bonus Questions: How does interest work in savings accounts? On credit cards? What's the difference between the two?

Score	
8-10	Donald Trump would be proud
6-7	Mini-mogul
4-5	Code blue
3-2	You're fired
1-0	Epic Fail

Mom, What's a Budget?

There are many important financial lessons parents know to impart to their teens by the time they are in high school. Budgets are like diets—nobody likes them, but people benefit when one is in place. Planning and limiting what is spent takes discipline and foresight, two traits not generally associated with teenage development. It has to start somewhere, so start with the financial literacy quiz. How did they do? How did *you* do? We can't teach what we don't know, but they don't have to know you Googled a few facts before going over this with them. Every teacher needs the key sometimes.

Ultimately, in our society most workers trade time for money. Since time is, in the end, all any of us really has in this life, the precious commodity of our minutes on this earth must be carefully weighed against the benefits of what the resulting pay brings. We need to make this as tangible as possible, since so much of the infrastructure of their lives has been invisibly rolled into our home budgets as they've grown up.

Even seemingly little things are easily taken for granted—like electricity, gas, and trash service—but each has a price tag. Do they know the difference between the cost of a cup of coffee made at home and at Starbucks? Place that in context by dividing it into the minimum wage and they'll have a new respect for the value of time.

Six Sick Challenges

Try on these six challenges for size:

1. **The One-Week Dining Solo Challenge.** Hand them $75 on a weekend afternoon and take them to the grocery store. Show them unit pricing on the labels of the shelves, and help them become educated consumers. How many servings of each item can help them stretch that money as far as possible? No restaurants allowed, and packed lunches only. With careful shopping, they should be able to make that stretch a full seven days in feeding themselves. If they make it at least 5 they're doing okay but will no doubt have developed a new appreciation for careful home economics budgeting. Less than 5 days, and they are heading for a pricey way of life that they themselves will need to somehow support.

2. **The Future Me Challenge.** Have your teen pick a career, and determine the cost of the number of years of college to attain it. Then—have them calculate what the monthly income would be for that job (after taxes). Invest $25 in a Monopoly game if you don't already have one (perhaps like me you remember this from a great episode of *The Cosby Show*). Sort out the money and actually hand it to them. Subtract each expense based on their desired adult lifestyle. Then present real-life scenarios and tradeoffs at them— helping a family member cover costs for an unexpected illness versus taking an extravagant vacation, etc. The tough choices adults have to make every day will begin crystallizing in the teen's mind, as they realize the power of money.

3. **The Banking Challenge #1.** Take your teen to your local bank branch and have them open a checking account if they don't already have one. Establish at least one monthly bill that they will be responsible for—even it is just $25 due toward their data usage on the iPhone that is surgically attached to them at all times. If they don't have a job, establish enough allowance to cover it, with chores to justify the income. Paying some bills on their own now develops crucial anticipatory skills. Walk them through balancing that checkbook.

4. **The Banking Challenge #2.** If your own credit is up to par, and you're feeling brave, consider co-signing on a credit card with a modest limit (just be sure to carefully monitor their spending). Credit cards are the bane of many American adults' existence, primarily because of ignorance about interest rates.

5. **The Retirement Challenge.** Have your teen calculate the year in which they plan to retire. For my 14 year old, this will be in the year 2063. Now, have them calculate the amount of savings they plan to set aside for each decade from 20-30, 30-40, 40-50, and 50+. Show them the amazing benefits of starting early and letting their money compound. With Social Security in its current state, if they don't want to eat cat food as a senior citizen, now is the time to make a long-term plan. Be sure they understand simple interest and compound interest are not just a chapter in their math books or a question on an SAT, but a real-life concept that can make or break their quality of life.

6. **The Plan Ahead Challenge.** The next time your teen asks for money for a new purchase, event, or trip help them set up a savings or debt plan to buy it for themselves. Eventually we all have to get off the gravy train, weaning them now is kinder than abruptly cutting them off entirely (or as I heard one father did, simply show them the door the day they turned 18 with a "good luck" and "don't come back.")

By incorporating these types of experiences into a teen's life, parents become an important resource for information, and create the bridge from financial dependency to independence. Why allow them to become a statistic, just another person with a poor credit history due to bad decisions based on ignorance?

Teens need to realize that missed payments are retained on a credit history for seven years, and that the wrong moves now can hurt them far down the road. Even seemingly inconsequential things like unpaid parking tickets can be a factor, and ramp up the interest rates they might be offered on something like an auto loan. This ties to the development of their character as well as their financial acumen. Our financial system rewards people who live within or below their means, who mean what they say, and sign agreements with integrity.

Taxes for Teens

Maybe you're like me, and can vividly remember the confusion, the anger, the fist-waving fury of that first paycheck when you were a teenager. I remember mine like it was yesterday. Having grown up in quaint small town America, I did what any girl would, and took a job at McDonald's on the main strip of town the day I turned 16 and was legally allowed to work. I made a measly $3.65 an hour, most of which I saved to pay back my father and granddad for the bright yellow 1969 Nash Rambler they'd bought me at auction as a repossession from the local telephone company. The windshield wipers didn't work, so when it rained, I had to stick my left arm out the window and manually clear the windshield, but to me it was a chariot of freedom. And it was a chariot I needed $575 to slowly reimburse them for from my income. The tally was written in magic marker on the wooden wall of my granddad's garage. "Pam's car," it said. My first possession, my greatest joy—and it took most of my junior year to afford.

I worked for two weeks in that lime green polyester pantsuit, complete with white visor and nametag. We had just gotten this newfangled thing called a drive-thru window, and I was designated as one of the first drive-thru girls. On Friday nights, the line of cars circled the golden arches and spit out down Centreville Road. "Hey Pam, give me some free fries!" friends would tease as I'd try to guess their names from the voices before telling them to "please drive around" in my then-southern drawl. Heady stuff for a country kid. I felt like a rock star.

When I saw that money had been taken out, I felt robbed. Abused. Mortified. "It's not fair!" I remember shouting. My dad just shook his head and smiled while my mom continued dinner in our 1970s kitchen. To add insult to injury, not only had the federal government robbed part of my precious $81, but the state had, too. I had no idea that American companies were and are required by law to take this money out of all employees' pay.

Your teen may not know the facts of life either. Oh sure, they know *those* facts of life, but not the ones that can significantly alter their lifestyle for better or for worse. It's time to break it to them gently.

Here are the most significant things to explain to a teenager to help them understand the American taxation process:

1. **Teach them about what the government does with taxes.** There are many great websites out there with information on both the federal and state level. Seeing it in pie charts, data graphs, and lists can really bring into sharp focus some things that your teen has probably never stopped to consider. For example, who do they think keeps the roads paved and the water in your community clean? No doubt, you will hear their dismay as they do a bit of research about excessive spending by the government, mismanagement, etc. That is good— it means they are becoming aware of the importance of our political process and the critical impact their participation can have both economically and in the political landscape.

2. **Whether they are a minor or not, every worker in America must pay taxes.** Age makes no difference to Uncle Sam in determining whether or not a person has to pay income tax. If your teen gets paid, the company is legally obligated to take taxes from their income. If they make over a certain amount in a given year, they will have to file. Explain to them what this means! For the 2012 tax year, the rules were as follows:

   a. Earned income of $5,950 or more requires them to file.

   b. If they earned interest on their savings account, or had other "unearned income" they will have to file if they made over $950.

   c. In the event they made a combination of earned and unearned income, things get complicated. Best thing to do is go online and look up IRS Publication 929.

   d. There may be times when teens don't have to file an income tax form, but it may benefit them to do so anyway. For example, if they worked part time for a company, only earned a small amount, and federal income taxes were taken out of that small amount, they would be due a refund and can only get their refund if they file an income tax form.

3. **Paperwork.** Go online together, and show them a few tax forms. Here are the main ones they need to understand:

   a. When your teenager gets a job, they will need to be able to fill out a W-4 form. You probably won't be there. Make sure they know what to expect before they start their job. ("What's a dependent, mom?")

b. At the beginning of the next year, they will receive their W-2 form. Be sure they know the importance of saving this form. Some parents even tuck it away for safekeeping. If it is lost, replacement is time consuming and potentially embarrassing.

c. Any self-employment work, such as mowing lawns or babysitting goes onto a Schedule C form.

4. **Responsibilities, even for babysitters and lawn helpers.** Each year, the US government sets a threshold amount for self-employment that doesn't have to owe taxes. In 2011, any amount over $400.00 was legally taxable. This is where you really have an opportunity to teach your teen about the ethics of taxation. Although they might not get caught if they don't report it, do you really want to send them the message that feigning ignorance is appropriate? Parents need to encourage their teens to keep track of their income, whether on an informal paper ledger or on the family computer. Depending on how many Friday and Saturday nights they are babysitting for $7 an hour, or how many lawns they mow, they can easily hit the government's tripping point for taxes owed. Helping them stand up to their legal and ethical obligations now can help create conscious, contributing citizens for life.

Credit Ratings and Your Teen

As adults we all know that having a solid credit score is often the single most important aspect of a person's financial life. These numbers, typically falling between 600 and 850, dictate major purchasing options in every young adult's life. Sadly, most teens don't even know what one is, much less how to get one.

Reasons this simple number can make or break your teenager in the near future:

1. They are more likely to be chosen by a landlord or boss to rent an apartment or get a job.
2. They can save significant thousands of dollars in interest payments on everything from a home loan to a car loan to credit card debt.
3. They can minimize the price of auto insurance premiums.
4. They can gain access to the most competitive rates on everything from cable service to their cell phone.

The real catch in getting a solid credit rating is the same for teens and adults—the way we build a credit history is by taking out loans and paying them on time; however, this isn't usually allowed without a credit history. What's a teen to do when they're new to the credit game?

Delayed Gratification

I'll gladly pay you Tuesday for a hamburger today.
　　　　　　—Wimpy, in the Popeye cartoons

If you're like me, you've chuckled at the humor behind this cartoon example of shortsighted credit seeking. Part of what's funny is that we realize he is not thinking at all about the end result of debt, he is merely focused on his appetite for a nice dinner. Like Wimpy, our teens can be tempted to go for the short-term satisfaction of getting something they want or have convinced themselves they "need," when the long-term consequences have not been thoroughly considered.

Although it can be tempting to say yes to every exploitative credit card that shows up in the mailbox, offering 19.99% to 24.99% APR for teens getting ready to go to college, all credit history is not helpful. Knowing when to say no is just as important as targeting the right "yeses." The goal has to be establishing solid credit, not just a credit history. Teens need parents who caution them to pause twice before borrowing once. The impact on their long-term financial future, and possibly yours, depends on it.

Credit scores are comprised of many aspects of a consumer's life. While there are many credit scoring formulas, they all look at roughly the same things. The most commonly used formula is known as a FICO score. Many factors contribute to the final number:

- 35% payment history
- 30% amounts owed
- 15% length of credit history
- 10% new credit
- 10% types of credit used

Note that the number one element in your teen's credit history will be their payment history. Explain to them that making payments on time is so important it merits a special pop up reminder on their iPhone's calendar app, a post-it note on their computer, or some other way of double-checking to ensure nothing is forgotten.

Be sure they know to allow for mailing times of up to a week or more if sending physical payments—mailing on the 30th and the due date being the 30th are two different things entirely, especially if the teen is in Dallas and the payment center is in Seattle. They should notice, too, that the second most important element is a ratio: how much they owe compared with how much credit they have available.

How can you help your teen understand this concept? Imagine they have a credit card with a $1,000 credit limit. On it they have a $300 balance. Your debt to credit would be:

$$300 \div 1,000 = 0.30 \text{ ratio, a.k.a } 30\% \text{ utilization}$$

Of course, this one is simplistic, but for more complicated numbers here's how they would figure out the debt to credit ratio with a calculator: enter the amount of the balance due; divide it by the amount of the credit limit (or in the case of a loan, the original starting amount). That is all it takes to calculate this important ratio.

What's a great ratio look like? Put it this way—those with FICO scores as high as 760 to 850 have bragging rights to an average debt to credit ratio of only 7%. A nice trick if you can get it. The issue is, and the credit card companies seem to know it, most young people launching out need to use as much of the credit they are given as possible to pay for everything from college to the car they plan to drive there. This can spell disaster, and start them down a dangerous road. Let's caution our teens that a smart consumer is a lousy credit card customer. Let's teach them to work the system to pay as few fees and little interest as possible.

Help Your Teen Establish a Payment History

Nowadays people know the price of everything and the value of nothing.

—Oscar Wilde

Let's look at some ways you can help your teen understand the value as well as the price of self-sustenance.

Savings and Checking Accounts
If they haven't already, have your teen open both a savings and a checking account in their own name. By regularly depositing and withdrawing money, and always being careful never to overdraw an account, they will demonstrate responsibility to the bank. Now, your teen's financial history with the bank doesn't usually directly affect their credit score unless an account gets overdrawn. But once they have shown a bank financial responsibility, they can apply for …. (drum roll, please…)

Low-Limit Credit Cards
Low-limit credit cards are given through banks with which consumers have an established relationship. By obtaining a credit card on the strength of their history with the bank for even a year or so, the teenager can begin to reap immediate benefits of taking the right actions. This initial step can lead to the second step, which is properly navigating usage of the first credit card in their own names.

Secured Loans

If your teen can't or prefers not to take out a credit card through the bank, consider having them apply for a secured loan that is well within their means to pay back fully and on time. A secured loan resembles an auto loan, so the bank will ask for some collateral in case they fail to pay. This makes it easier to qualify for the loan.

Secured Credit Cards

Secured credit cards can be used just like unsecured cards, but teens have to put down a security deposit as collateral. They're probably the best place to start when it comes to establishing credit, since banks give them liberally, even with no credit history. For example, have them save $300, then deposit it into a secured Visa or MasterCard. Their credit line will start off matching what was already deposited, but over time will increase. As they use and pay off the card responsibly, they eventually get the deposit back and raise the credit limit—all while building a great credit history. One caveat: some banks offer these only with dreadful terms, including high fees, so help your teen read the fine print carefully.

Utilities

Did you know that one way your teen can establish a payment history is through utilities? It does not all have to happen through credit cards or loans. According to the FTC, utility payments like phone, water, electricity and natural gas are allowed to impact credit ratings. This makes sense when you remember that each of these forms of "credit" involves getting services now and paying for them later.

Utility credit is usually much easier to get than most other types of credit, so consider moving certain utilities into your teen's name if they aren't already—for example, by purchasing their own cell phone plan. If they live on their own, make sure that necessary utilities are in their own names, not yours. Allow them to shoulder the necessary responsibilities that come along with so-called freedom.

Once anything is in their name, make sure their payments are on time, every time by checking in with them for the first few months in case they let it slip. It is easy to do and common for young adults to get so distracted by jobs, classes and their social lives that they let things slide without even realizing it. By the time they do, it could be too late and they could be in a hole that requires escaping.

Chapter 9

COLLEGE QUEST

Seven years of college down the drain.
—John Blutarski (John Belushi), *Animal House*

A*nimal House* is one of the raunchiest (and funniest) movies I was allowed to see when I was in high school. I remember thinking, *Wow, I wonder if college is really like that*—crazy deans, wild parties, and John Belushi starting food fights in the cafeteria. Although I never saw a single toga in all my time at Columbia, I did have a lot of fun, and also managed to do something that even those misguided characters in the movie did: I learned some things. Here for you is a list of important considerations for parents to keep in mind, in order to not make some pretty common mistakes.

Student Debt

One of the primary hurdles in gaining financial independence for young Americans today is the siren song of amassing college loans. Oh sure, they sound so pretty, singing from the rocks as they lure families into signing over promissory notes for interest rates they feel inconsequential at the time, but many a young adult has been shipwrecked on the rocks when they hit their career years and can barely make ends meet due to all that debt. Whether the funds came through the federal government, through friends and family, through lending institutions or through the university itself, college debt has become a dangerous habit. With the need for higher education a given in so many fields of expertise, what's a parent to do?

As of this writing, the outstanding American student debt is valued at nearly $1.2 trillion. Many teens can't even accurately write that number, much less comprehend the implications for the economic structure they are inheriting—but indebted families trying to spend, invest and save less in order to pay off student loans can wreck havoc on the flow of commerce in this country.

Experts caution to consider the amount being borrowed, and to refinance any loan to more affordable terms if it seems unruly to pay in comparison with other options. Some legwork and inquiry will be necessary to shepherd your teen through the gauntlet, but this is a critical time to be sure they aren't being set up for failure a few short years down the road. Young adults will need funds to buy homes, start businesses, and contribute to their communities. The freer of debt they are as they start that new chapter, the better.

On average, new college graduates' $25,000 -$30,000+ in debt marks a major shift in American economy. Parents need to ensure their teens are able to buy their first car or afford their first home when the time comes by helping them make smart decisions in paying for their college educations. As of July 2012, about 60% of all federal student loans carried interest rates above 6%, according to the US Department of Education. About three-quarters of all new federal student loans carried interest rates of 6.8% or 7.9%, forcing borrowers to pay record relative rates on their loans. What a nightmare for a young person trying to build a future for themselves. It's hard to fly with an anvil around your ankle. See Sam Mikhail's bonus chapter in this book for detailed, expert advice on how to solve this dilemma.

In State or Out of State?

Location, location, location. The comedic saying about the three most important factors in choosing real estate aptly applies to the college search as well. Whether your teen will begin in a local community college and transfer to a 4-year institution from there, or leap right into the thick of university life months after high school graduation—having the right facts in place creates crucial context for decisions that carry both short-term and long-term consequences.

Out-of-state schools almost always seem to sock it to your wallet much harder than those in state, at least on the surface. Be aware, though, that some schools are more generous with aid than others, so the "ticket price" isn't as set in stone as you might first think. Do your research!

Even with an added cost, certain schools are sometimes justifiable depending upon the match between their program offerings and your teenager. The economic principle of ROI—return on investment—should be the guiding principle. How much of what your teen will gain at that school will impact or determine their subsequent opportunities?

Really Great Reasons to Stay In State

There are terrific advantages to students choosing to attend an in-state university, both logistic and financial. Practically speaking, if you send them out of state you can plan on paying for round trip airfare at least twice a year, and often more during the freshman transition. Staying in state often means a few tanks of gas rather than a huge credit card debt to an airline. By living close to home, say within a two-hour drive, students have the option to go home more often than out-of-state students since it doesn't involve plane fare, a train ticket, or a long drive.

In terms of financial advantage, depending on what endowments exist for schools in your state, your student may be eligible for both merit-based scholarships and grants by staying close to home. Keeping them closer to home can also save those widely known fees and expenses added to full-freight tuition incurred by going out-of-state. Just be aware that some schools are notoriously stingy while others are generous with aid—gather lots of data before assuming anything.

Many young adults today simply forego the entire separation issue, and live at home with mom and dad while attending college either full-time or part-time. Needless to say, this creates challenges. What is a fair portion of responsibility for your son or daughter to bear? Should they pay rent and/or contribute to the grocery bill? Whatever you decide, beware of the tendency to simply continue business as usual. No self-respecting 20 year-old has mom doing his laundry and making his dinner every night. Shades of independence need to be factored into the "new arrangement," even when they have been sleeping in the same twin bed since elementary school.

The level of competition your teen faces when applying for out-of-state colleges increases, because many schools target a particular quota for the number of out-of-state students they are willing to admit. Despite certain exceptions, state schools are often more generous with their own taxpayers' students than they are with outsiders. Public colleges save their money for in-state students—so use this to your advantage and find those in your home state that might ease the financial strain simply because of your zip code.

Moving to another state can be terrifying for some teenagers. No matter how they've longed for freedom, and counted down days to "getting out of prison" to embark on their new lives, when push comes to shove they can get cold feet. College is already a huge adjustment in and of itself, and factoring in the drastic change of a cross-country move is simply more than some teens can manage. Separation anxiety is all too real for some, varying in degree from mild discomfort to pure panic.

Now: no amount of financial advantage for staying in-state can balance the wrong fit in these critical areas for your teen to enjoy their quality of life. They are already having to wean off of a level of comfort and dependency on home and parents, so don't make it any harder on him or her by sending your sun-loving surfer off to University of Vermont. Just make sure the school offers merits from each of the following perspectives: offering the right major, strong reputation for professors, comfortable average student-teacher ratio and class size, social opportunities, physical environment with weather and amenities your student loves.

If they'd rather be away but have to stay in state for financial reasons, make the most of it. They can still live on campus to get some independence. They can still get involved in campus life—by joining clubs and organizations, they will meet likeminded people from different backgrounds. When those students are from different parts of the country or world, it can make even their hometown feel exotic.

Also: have them look into the study abroad program. Sometimes these can be surprisingly affordable, and offer travel opportunities that change lives for the better and define career choices. Just be aware that many of them fall in love with a country (or someone in it) and don't want to come home. My own sister fell in love with an Italian while abroad at the age of 19, and I have a bilingual niece and nephew to prove it.

Really Great Reasons for Going Out of State

College is a great time for students to seek new horizons, to break away from old habits and to re-evaluate hometown norms. When they stay put, the temptation to congregate with the same peers at the same places can inhibit their growth socially and psychologically. Some students who begin their freshman year at or near home quickly realize the thrill is gone and they need to venture forth. Restlessness is not uncommon, and the need to travel and expand marks a healthy transition to young adulthood.

Informed parents recognize that choosing an out-of-state school can give their teen the opportunity to live in a new place and experience new a lifestyle. Bringing all they are and have learned in their first 18 years out into the broader world can be exhilarating for young adults. How can they verify and validate who they are without anything to compare it to? Think about it—if they live in a dorm, they will be able to experience a whole new environment within the constraints of a relatively stable and secure infrastructure. Why not let them experience a new location too? With their food plan in the college cafeteria, campus housing and transportation in place, they can fly "solo" with lots of peripheral protection in place—happy circumstances for protective mamas and papas.

Sending your teen out of state provides them with a relatively safe way to explore. Regardless of where they attend, they can venture forth with the safety net of the family still intact back home. If they happen to discover their choice isn't working out, you can provide a safe place to regroup. This is not uncommon among first-semester freshmen. I've seen instances where the student went to an out-of-state college, flew home for Thanksgiving break, and didn't want to return to the school. The parents had to prevail in getting them to finish out the semester or lose all tuition since the dropping deadline had long ago passed.

Another benefit is the anonymity being far from home provides. Some teens have become notorious by the time they hit 18—whether through reputation as a party animal, a shy brainy science geek, or a supposedly dumb jock, those assumptions and reputations can inhibit their ability to step into the fullness of a new self. Like a snake shedding its skin, they need a place to wriggle out of the old ways. Heading out of state can be their big chance to make a clean break of it. The freedom to reinvent, and be whomever they decide to become without familiar acquaintances questioning it, can be quite liberating.

Advantages come with the varied academic options and types of programs offered by particular schools throughout the country. By casting as broad a net as possible, and working together to explore all the possibilities—whether alone on the Internet or with the help of a guidance counselor or educational professional— your teen can truly gather the best of the best in terms of working toward specific career goals. Be aware that some state school systems, such as North Carolina and California, are somewhat notorious for being difficult to get into for students who live out-of-state. Knowing the admissions policies and history of particular schools will guide you and your student to invest your time and efforts in the most productive way possible.

Particular majors and special programs predominate at certain colleges—and this could also influence your teen's decision to leave his or her home state. Most families know to begin gathering information as early as the sophomore year of high school. Those who wait to begin until late in the junior year, or heaven forbid the senior year, have really missed the boat.

Name-Brand Schools: The Cult of Prestige

All college degrees are not created equal. The employer your little darling hopes to impress in five years will no doubt have a stack of resumes to sift through. A designer label on clothing or shoes simply impresses some people, and the same holds true for colleges. Without debating the reasons why or the ethics of the matter, if a parent wants their student to be competitive, they need to at least consider the difference between the perceived value of Generic U. on a resume with that of a widely and recognizably respected institution. Why do you think all those wealthy families are willing to pay into the six figures annually for their progeny to attend top schools? Answer: because they know it can be worth the investment, and they can afford it.

Fact: the annual tuition for undergraduates attending Columbia University in the City of New York in 2013 was $49,259. By contrast, one university in Oregon charged $6,639 for both in-state and out-of-state tuition (almost unheard of, which is why I mention it here). Certainly, moms and dads would love to pocket that $42,620. Over the course of four years, they could pay off over $170,000 on their home mortgage with that money, or take some really rad trips. But before you begin packing for Belize, stop and imagine your son or daughter's resume on that stack of job applicants. What kind of school diploma do you think is more likely to generate the phone call to come interview?

Your son or daughter might be perfect for the job, and few would argue that there is anything "fair" about this, but in a competitive job search, the perceived value of the name of an Alma Mater matters. Ponder the difference in perception between an Ivy League school and a small college in a low population area with little name recognition outside of its own geographic region. How much is the smart-by-association prestige of a degree from a top college worth to you and your family?

The common wisdom among many college consultants is that students should apply to 8-12 schools—4 targets, 4 safeties, and 4 stretches. You can determine your teen's likelihood of admission by consulting most universities' admissions pages on their websites. Look at the range of SAT/ACT scores, GPAs, and other factors. If they are in range it is a target school, is they are above, some would call that a safety (although in today's competitive academic environment, one could argue there is no such thing as a surely "safe" school anymore). If the teen's scores fall below the range, that school is considered a stretch. Perhaps athletic or artistic contributions they can potentially make to campus life (i.e.; in the band) will increase their likelihood of acceptance, as will fortuitous facts like family member alumni. This is an art of approximation, not a science, but let common sense guide in assessing how your student will fare among likely applicants.

You can also look at acceptance rates. Stanford University accepted only 7% of the applying students in the 2012–13 school year. Those types of statistics should give you pause before even placing them as a "stretch" on your teen's list. After all, most college applications require many hours of time and fees ranging from $40 to $100 per application, unless students are eligible for a fee waiver. Even with these waivers, the time factor can escalate quickly. Anyone who helps juniors and seniors in high school will attest: each form, each recommendation letter, each essay requirement, and each fee can take its toll. Multiply that by 8, 10, or 12 schools and add it to a course load already filled with heavy homework demands—not to mention extracurricular and athletic endeavors—and you've got a recipe for what I call the midyear meltdown.

One strategy that works well for parents and teens who aren't sure where to aim is to apply to schools with a variety of locations and descriptions. If you add to this target-safety-stretch list the factor of in state versus out of state—your target list might look something like this:

- Two in-state target colleges
- Two out-of-state target colleges
- Two in-state safety colleges
- Two out-of-state safety colleges
- Two in-state stretch colleges
- Two out-of-state stretch colleges

The Boomerang Generation

Fostering financial independence in a teenager is an art form not for the faint of heart (or wallet). Did you know that the so-called "boomerang generation," those currently 25 to 34 years old, more and more frequently end up living with their parents? This is because they can't make ends meet on their own.

According to a recent Pew study, the percentage of middle-aged parents who provide primary financial support for a child over the age of 18 has increased from 20% to 27% since 2005.

An additional 21% of parents say they provide "some support" for their adult kids. Some in the media have nicknamed these parents as "baby-gloomers." In today's economy, it takes purposeful strategies to ensure financial independence for our children.

Lack of motivation is not the culprit, since so many young adults truly long for greater financial and logistic independence, but escalating college costs, limited job prospects in many fields, and the high cost of living all loom as bogeymen. When our children were young, we could assure them there were no monsters in the closet, but now that they are becoming young adults, they face actual dangers—many of them financial.

What is truly alarming is how many teens have a poor or minimal understanding of budgeting and basic finance. Do you really want to pay for your adult children to have smart phones, Internet access, iTunes and Hulu? This is becoming the norm for many families, creating an enfeebled generation. A Wall Street Journal survey of parents with adult children up to 35 years old found that more than 40% still pay for their kids' cell phone service. We all want our adult kids to call home, but at what point is this dependency inappropriate?

As recommended in the last chapter, ask your teen how much they know about personal finance issues. Typically, about 25% admit they don't understand how to budget, 20% don't understand how to establish and protect their credit, and about a third don't have a clue about how to invest money. Now is the time to create time together to teach them skills they need for life. For example, ask them what they know about taxes. You might be surprised at how little their schools have explained. Most can rattle off the Pythagorean theorem, and formulas for the area of a circle, square and trapezoid—yet they haven't a clue about the real-life math needed to thrive in our society.

The cost of college—and the fact that today's teens are unprepared to contribute to those expenses—is one reason they might be inhabiting your basement into their mid-20s. The percentage of Americans who can't pay back their student loans has spiked incredibly, and the cost of higher education isn't getting any cheaper. In fact, the average debt student borrowers accrue has jumped 30% in five years and now averages over $24,000? Ouch!

Since forgoing higher education isn't really a viable option, what's a parent to do? Think about carving out time to talk with your teen about present and future expectations for their financial growth toward independence. Chances are, they're pretty scared, so be ready to help them navigate the fog with your adult perspective. Sometimes car trips provide a great neutral environment for this, rather than the formality of a face-to-face. "So, Jonathan, you're almost a senior. Have you thought about establishing a credit rating? Would you like me to help you with that?" or "Samantha, I've noticed your cell phone and data costs are averaging over $100 a month now. At what point do you think it's fair to contribute to those expenses?" or "That college you're looking at runs about $20,000 a year, honey. Dad and I can pitch in about $5,500 of that. We'd like you to take the lead in finding scholarships through your school's college counselor, and let us know how we can support you. Okay?"

Avoiding these discussions now is tempting but unfair. We don't help our teens at all by perpetuating the illusion that money will always magically be there. The sooner we help them think like adults with a plan, the better.

With any luck, the boomerang won't pop back. Frisbees are so much more fun anyway, don't you agree?

HOW TO KEEP YOUR TEEN SAFE ON CAMPUS

Dan Magnus

A note about the contributing author: Dan Magnus is a two-time world kickboxing champion with a roster of celebrity clients, and the colleague I trust to train my family in personal defense.

E ach person has his or her own unique personality—I, myself, have a hero syndrome. I live to help, fix or save people with problems. I guess I read too many superhero stories as a child. This brings me to what *The M.A.G.N.U.S. Method* is all about. I use my own name as an acronym—I like to use acronyms when I teach people, because for some reason they tend to stick.

M stands for *Mindset*. Each teenager holds a particular mindset about life. I recommend you help them develop a defensive mindset if they don't already have one. Hopefully they'll never need it, but what if they do? As a professional bodyguard, I'm constantly looking for signs that something is out of the ordinary. No one can always be prepared for something bad to happen, but I've trained my mind to respond quickly.

Your teen needs to have that mindset. I protect people, find people, save people and fix people. Most teens have scattered mindsets: one for work, another for play, and another for whatever else they do in life. That's normal, but teens need to always notice things happening around them, even when it interferes with their preferred happy, playful mindset. They don't need to have a worst-case scenario mindset like mine, but developing a mindset of awareness can save their lives.

That brings us to A. *Attitude*. Your teen's attitude is going to play a key role in whether they're going to avoid a dangerous situation or walk right into one. Their attitude or the way they typically act plays a key role in how people see them. Others tend to see my personal attitude as very dark. To strangers, it's a very "don't bother me, don't talk to me" attitude. It takes people time to realize that I'm not going to rip their heads off.

The job and lifestyle that I have created just projects a perceived attitude. I'm not mean to people, just indifferent. If your teen is an upbeat, social person and were to try to copy my attitude, they'd just look silly. In fact, they could make a bad situation worse. Their attitude must match their personality, but no matter what their personality type, they have to be taught to show that they're not going to be taken lightly if an adverse situation occurs.

Next is G. *Guts*. Does your teen have the guts to do what's necessary to end a conflict? No, I'm not just talking about self-defense techniques like punching and kicking. Most teens have never hit another person, much less injured another person. I'm talking about the number one technique I teach—having the guts to leave, run away, and get the heck out of there! That, my friends, can take guts because no one wants to feel like a coward. This happens more with men than women, but women also feel it.

Your teen must be taught: if you can get away, do it. Even if they think there's no way to get away, they must be encouraged to do what they can, even if it means severely injuring an assailant. They might think, "I can do it. I can stick my fingers into his eyes to blind him so I can get away." Chances are, no they can't. It's like the first time getting on a bicycle. They're scared to death, they fall down, and they have to practice over and over until both mind and body believe they can ride that bike. I'm not suggesting that you have your teens run around randomly attacking people for practice. But, be sure they get into their head that they may have to one day defend themselves if they can't get away. To do that takes both mental and physical training.

N is for *Negotiation*. In every type of conflict, there's some sort of negotiation. It can be long and drawn out like a hostage situation or one word: No! The idea of someone jumping out of the bushes, attacking and leaving without saying a word is pure fantasy, unless it's during a war. Even if that person comes out of nowhere, words will be spoken. Words can be one of the strongest weapons humans have on this earth. Whoever said, "Sticks and stones may break my bones but words will never hurt me," must've been deaf. "Sticks and stones may break your bones, but words will destroy you," is much more accurate. If you can learn how to use words correctly, you can protect yourself and your loved ones better than any punch, kick, knife, gun, bomb or weapon.

It's all in the U. *Understanding*. Teens must be able to understand what is actually going on around them. How they see must be more acute than what they see. They must try to understand what is going on and how you are going to deal with it. When something bad happens, the tendency is to say, "Why, why is this happening to me?" They can get so caught up in why that they forget how it really happened. For example, it was late and they were parked on the lower level of a garage. Their car, and maybe a couple of other cars, were still down there. They noticed some men standing in the garage standing around, maybe just talking. Your teen wanted to get to their car, but was nervous about the three men. What did they do? Most would have continued walking toward the car, thinking, "If I get to the car, I'll be safe." Guess again. That car won't stop an attacker if they want to get them. In fact, it helps the attacker.

What they should have done is leave the garage. They should have used the technology that this world has now, their ever-present cell phone, and called the police. This is what police are for, not to stop crime, but to prevent it. Teach your teens that the police are a deterrent, not a solution. So, they should know they have the right to call the police. The police would have arrived and your teen would have told them what happened. The police would have escorted them to their car, and then found out why the three men are standing around. Let the police do their job; it's easier than them investigating someone's demise. Being more aware and understanding of their rights in the situation will keep your teen safer.

Finally, S stands for *Spirit*. Teach your teen to foster an indomitable spirit, to never quit, and to never give up. Simply believing in themselves and the power they possess gives them the edge against any predator. We're all prey, but it's our spirit that can caution the wrong people to back off. Does your teen's spirit come out strong, confident, and able? If not, it's time to help them work on it. People with strong spirits lead, but your teen needs to remember that there are both good and bad people with indomitable spirits. Can they tell the difference? If not, they need training to develop discernment.

Welcome to the human species. The world exists in controlled chaos, because most people have set tolerance levels for one another. Law enforcement was created as a deterrent to stop the public from doing whatever they desired. However, not everyone wants to obey laws. For years, I thought that I was stopping crime, but I realized that I was stopping criminals. It takes ordinary citizens to stop crime, or at least make it more difficult to cause crime. The more aware your teenager becomes, the harder it will be for a predator to commit a crime against them. Remember, criminals practice their craft too. Unfortunately, you and I will never completely stop crime, war or violence, but by raising awareness we can minimize their potentially lethal effects.

Checklist #3

FOR PHYSICAL INDEPENDENCE

🔑 Discuss the role of hygiene and physical appearance in attracting or repelling potential employers, professors, and friends

🔑 Laundry: hot is for whites, cold is for darks. Don't mix them
if you don't want everything you own to look dingy.
Not rocket science.

🔑 Get them moving and make sure they have a plan in place for physical activity in college.

🔑 Money: the root of all evil that makes the world go 'round. Teach taxes, credit ratings, and financial fluency, or be prepared to personally pay the price.

🔑 Use professional guidelines and/or college planners to make sure you are targeting the right colleges for your student. Don't assume they know anything—you'd be surprised how many teens choose a school simply because, "My friend wants to go there."

🔑 Get your kids to a self-defense course before sending them out into the world. Don't let them become another statistic.

Key #4

SPIRITUAL INDEPENDENCE

Chapter 10

GRACE

'Tis grace that brought me safe this far
And grace will lead me home.

—John Newton, "Amazing Grace"

Here is what I believe: our children are connected to the energy of all creation; they are part of it and it is part of them. They come to this world through us, but not from us. I no more knew who was about to be born each time I entered labor than I knew the man in the moon. The amazement of each unique baby, as I looked at her for the first time, reduced me to trembling and tears. How could such holiness have entered this world through my body? Ask any mom and she'll tell you— nothing on earth is more humbling.

You may be asking yourself why these chapters are dedicated to spiritual independence, so I'll tell you. In my 20+ years of experience as a mother and educator, I've witnessed a startling fact: aspects of life related to meaning, spirit, and context (the "why") define the separation between the merely successful and the truly joyful young adults. In fact, spiritual independence is central to happiness and therefore success.

Oprah Winfrey once said, "Spirituality is not religion. You can be spiritual and not have a religious context. The opposite is true too: You can be very religious with no spiritual dimension, just doctrine." She makes an excellent point—we are all spiritual beings having a human experience, not human beings lurching toward this thing outside of ourselves called "spirit." I love that the lyrics of "Amazing Grace," one of the most famous hymns of all time, don't say, "And God will lead me home." They say that grace will. I firmly believe that grace can lead our teens and us to our highest good, with or without an overtly religious paradigm in place.

I think making the ephemeral tangible is helpful, so let's say this—look into your teen's eyes. Can you see them in there—those little toddlers and infants they once were? Isn't it hard to imagine a time when they weren't already in your life? Yes, and the reason is because of this ineffable thing I am calling spirituality. I am not promoting belief in anything in particular. I am merely asking parents to pause, breathe, and notice the miraculous fact that teenagers are spiritual beings who need guidance to become independent in that area of their lives.

The Right to Decide

What, ultimately, do you believe is your responsibility in launching your young adult toward spiritual independence?

Notice this isn't a question about religion, but a larger matter. Spirituality recognizes the interdependence of all living things, and seeks connection. Whether you or your teen believe in God or not, no human being can escape the questions of the meaning and purpose of life—the "what's it all about, Alfie?" Everyone must come to whatever perspective they eventually embrace on their own.

I've noticed how annoyed most people get when someone proselytizes. No one likes to be bossed around, and teens are notoriously stubborn in this area. Faith can only be embraced or disavowed within the private contents of an individual's heart. I am reminded of the famous Norman Rockwell picture of a 1950s mother dressed for church, with a gaggle of young children falling in line behind her walking out the front door while dad hides behind his reading chair with his pipe and morning newspaper. Taking a 6-year-old to Sunday School sure is a lot easier than trying to compel a grown man to believe or behave the way that woman may have wanted him to.

So here we are, suspended in the gap between toddler and adult. Teens tend to ask questions that make parents nervous:

- If God is real, how come bad things happen to good people?
- How can I know if what others believe in is true?
- What if all I really know is that I have no idea about spirituality at all?

Some parents, particularly those with firm beliefs of their own, trust that taking their teens to church, synagogue or temple should be enough to ensure lifelong obedience to a similar belief system. For some families, this is indeed the case, as generation after generation joins the pews or prayer mats in the same house of worship. But more often than not, this is not the case.

Recent data attests that many if not most young adults pull away from what they've been taught. In February 2012, George Stephanopoulos interviewed Governor Rick Santorum, then-candidate for the Republican nomination for President. Santorum quipped, "You know the statistic . . . 62% of kids who enter college with some sort of faith commitment leave without it." Although many debated whether this number was inflated for political effect, the general perception holds among many communities today that young adults often wander from the paths of their parents.

Although it is understandable that parents want the apples that fall from their trees to embrace similar worldviews, trying to mandate such things has backfired for many a parent. Who doesn't know someone who irreverently calls himself or herself a "recovering Catholic" or "former Mormon?" Conversely, if a teenager blindly follows Mom or Dad through adulthood, and then veers irrevocably away from that predetermined spiritual path, does that mean mom or dad did something wrong? Or might they have done something right?

Multiculturalism as a Path to Independence

One suggestion I can make, which I've seen impact young adults positively, is the comparative study of religions as a shared family endeavor. Most public school classes completely avoid the topic of religion, and understandably so. Other schools that do address religion promote one particular view without a survey of alternative viewpoints. Interfaith education, when instituted in the early teen years by mindful parents, can incorporate visits to mosques, Sunday schools, synagogues, and Buddhist temples.

Parents could consider introducing Christian, Jewish, Hindu, and Buddhist studies as a group activity—maybe with visits to a local public library for books, with online web searches, and with seeking out speakers on You Tube or Ted Talks with something to say on the matter. Knowledge about other faiths can only enhance understanding, and peaceful coexistence becomes much more likely for future generations if we ensure our next generation of adults does a better job than we have at getting to know one another—in person. By putting a face to a community, humanizing a faith tradition can replace the typical assumptions and prejudices.

I grew up next door to my very religious grandmother, whom we all called Nanny. She only had an 8th-grade education, but she could quote chapter and verse of the Bible like a Jeopardy champion. When I was accepted to Columbia University, she asked what kind of classes I would be taking. I told her that there was a multi-cultural requirement, and that I looked forward to studying Buddhism, Hinduism, Islam, and aboriginal beliefs. Her face blanched. "Why would a nice Christian girl like you want to study those ol' devil religions?" she asked me in her country twang.

She was a wonderful, sweet woman, but she had grown up on a dirt floor on the Tennessee/Virginia state line in Appalachia. If it wasn't Pentecostal it wasn't kosher, so to speak. She couldn't tell you the first thing about Buddhism, or any other faith for that matter. She was not a bigot. Far from it—she was one of the kindest people you could ever meet. But she saw the world in blissful binaries, and that was a problem for someone like me. Although I loved her very much, I knew that any faith I hoped to have or hold would, for me, have to be refined in the fire of exploration of other traditions out there.

As fascinating as it was to grow up being brought to outdoor tent revival meetings in the summer, carrying my grandmother's tambourine under one arm and a fat Bible beneath the other, you can bet that my life's study of anthropology of world religions has served me. God bless her, as we say down south. And God rest her soul too. Nanny was one of the greatest teachers in my life.

Perhaps there is a lesson in this for other parents—we can't shut out 30% of the USA or 66% of the world's population. We can't only show our teens the parts that are congruent with our own beliefs. They are becoming world citizens, and if they're going to be ready for that, they need and deserve accurate information.

12 Steps for Parents of Teens

In addition to embracing multiculturalism, another suggestion I can make is that parents consider applying some or all of the 12 Steps of Alcoholics Anonymous to their parenting lives. The most time-honored spiritual principles of all history can be found in these 12 ideas, and these have been modified since the 1930s for many different audiences.

Although they were first conceived by a recently sobering doctor named Bob and his formerly chronic-drinking friend Bill W., programs all over the world use them now to apply to everything from addiction to sex to gambling to narcotics to shopping to self-injury to eating disorders and more. Those of us who have been affected by addiction in loved ones' lives use these steps in a program called Al Anon. Parents of teens deserve our own self-help program, so this seems an easy thing to apply to our lives.

Remarkably pliable, these 12 little nuggets of wisdom carry a special message. We may not be addicted to our teens, but we must overcome any delusion that we can live their lives for them now that they are launching towards adulthood, ready or not. Read these reworked versions of the 12 Steps, and see if you don't agree:

1. We admitted we were powerless over the outcome of our teen's life.

2. Came to believe that a higher power than ourselves could shepherd them to their highest purpose.

3. Made a decision to turn their lives over to the care of a loving higher power.

4. Made a searching and fearless moral inventory of ourselves, resolving to improve our own spiritual clarity in order to better parent our teen.

5. Admitted to God, to ourselves, and to our teen the exact nature of enough of our own human failings to demonstrate both humility and vulnerability.

6. Were entirely ready to let go of all characteristics that undermine our usefulness to our teens and others.

7. Humbly asked our higher power to remove our shortcomings and guide us as parents.

8. Made a list of any harm we have caused, and became willing to make amends to our teen and others.

9. Made direct amends wherever possible, within appropriate boundaries of discretion and divulging.

10. Continued to take personal inventory, and when we were wrong, promptly admitted it.

11. Sought to improve our conscious contact on our spiritual path, praying diligently for our teens (and ourselves) to have knowledge of our unique, divine purpose and the power to carry that out.

12. Having had a spiritual awakening as the result of these steps, we tried to carry this message to other parents of teens, and to practice these principles in all our affairs.

"What an order; I can't go through with it!" shout the attendees at many 12-step programs immediately after their programs' version of these steps are read aloud. You know what happens next? Laughter erupts—because everyone knows that perfection is not the point, progress is.

Nobody loves hypocrisy. Saying what you mean, and meaning what you say, is one of the central values of almost all civilized societies. Yet, the notion of walking the walk—not just talking the talk—can be elusive. Teens benefit from explicit dialogue with the adults in their lives about the notion of congruency. This ideal, of having our insides match our outsides, is easier said than accomplished. Sometimes, folks need to "fake it 'til they make it." As the old cliché reminds us, you can't judge a book by its cover. When teens compare their inside states of being to the outside appearances of others, trouble's ahead. The 12 steps can provide an elegant way for parents to individuate with grace as their teens move ahead into adulthood.

Holy Wholeness—Or, Wholly Holy

This is my favorite quote of all time, by Marianne Williamson. "Our deepest fear is not that we are inadequate. Our deepest fear is that we are powerful beyond measure. It is our light, not our darkness that most frightens us. We ask ourselves, 'Who am I to be brilliant, gorgeous, talented, and fabulous?' Actually, who are you *not* to be? You are a child of God. Your playing small does not serve the world." How's that for a pep talk the next time you or your teen feel weak or frightened?

Some people want to be holy; others just want to be whole. Even our word "holiday" contains the idea of that which is holy. This Germanic word, related to the Latin *sanctus*, means sacred, whole, intact. What parents do well to consider are the personal responsibilities we bear for manifesting holiness—"wholeness"—in our teen's lives. I'm not talking about making them become religiously aligned. I'm talking about helping them evolve into morally alert, ethically conscious beings.

I would argue that both our children and our holidays are holy whole in proportion to our intention to help them manifest that quality in their lives. Our entire post-modern, deconstructivist era seems bent on separating things, investigating them, and sometimes missing the larger picture. Our teens are not simply a list of aspects and adjectives, they are so utterly complex that any honest parent will readily admit we haven't the foggiest clue how it all came together and now marches around our homes in hipster apparel.

The demands of our high tech, lowbrow culture really complicates this notion of seeking holiness. As members of a capitalist society, we are inundated with images and messages seemingly bent upon making us question every follicle of hair on our misbegotten heads in order to sell us this product or that. The nerve-wracking fallout is that teens can sometimes be inured to caring about human vulnerability and connection before they even leave home. As long as they look right, some embrace a fake "swagger"—a pseudo self-confidence that can rot them from the inside out if they're not careful. The problem with stuff—things, products, devices, and fashion—is that stuff cannot and does not replace the human need to be seen, heard, loved, and accepted. How can we as parents help bridge this gap?

I bet you know people who love Christmas but avoid the deeper mysteries of the season. After all, it's so much easier to buy a plastic tree than to cut down a real one, and much harder to fathom a virgin birth than a fat bearded Santa at a mall. Holidays become holy days only when we bring that intention to them.

Perhaps the most challenging aspect of this for teens, and many adults, is the requisite quiet and self-reflection needed to make "room in the Inn" of our own hearts to allow something divine to enter in. It can feel isolating to get quiet like that, and in our teenagers' world of constant stimulation—where a 6-second Vine constitutes an important creative expression—remaining fractured looms as more likely than integrating through deliberately embracing a higher, more wholly authentic, self.

Marianne Williamson reminds her readers that, "According to the mystical tradition, Christ is born into the world through each of us. As we open our hearts, he is born into the world. As we choose to forgive, he is born into the world … who we're capable of being emerges into the world, and weaknesses of the former self begin to fade."

The objective of wholeness requires letting go of many patterns of thinking that easily corrode the joy our teenagers might otherwise find in their lives. They must reject blame to seek harmony, avoid gossip to respect privacy, let go of dwelling on perceived problems to find solutions. In short, they must be willing to be a blessing to others by first blessing themselves.

I love that Williamson asserts that Christ "…is in a state that is still potential in the rest of us. The image of Jesus has been so perverted, so twisted by institutions claiming to represent him. As it's stated in the *Course in Miracles*, 'Some bitter idols have been made of him who came only to be brother to the world.'"

Every one of us must filter our perception of the container for holiness through our own cultures and life experiences. What our teens need is to find their way on the path toward becoming whole by understanding why it matters. Whether they are Catholic, Protestant, Mormon, Muslim, Buddhist, Jewish, Hindu, agnostic, pagan or atheist, cultivating the quiet space within as they seek and find their way can offer true comfort and light for the paths ahead they must tread without us.

And so, the final word goes back to Marianne Williamson, who has spent her career breaking down spiritual principals in ways that regular folks can understand: "There is nothing enlightened about shrinking so that other people will not feel insecure around you. We are all meant to shine, as children do. We were born to make manifest the glory of God that is within us. It is not just in some of us; it is in everyone. And as we let our own light shine, we unconsciously give others permission to do the same. As we are liberated from our own fear, our presence automatically liberates others." All I can say to that is Amen, sister.

Chapter 11

TOOLS

Tool 1: Giving Them the Freedom to Explore

Freedom is not worth having if it does not connote the freedom to err.

—Mahatma Gandhi

The goal for parents must be to equip their child with tools to develop their own active, vibrant relationship to the world around them—with or without the accoutrement of familial traditions. This is an area I know well, both as a daughter and a mom. I am the firstborn child of a devout Catholic mother, yet I become a non-denominational Christian at the age of 17, somewhat to the dismay of my truly wonderful mother.

A deep empathy for how she must have felt emerged within me when my own firstborn, as she became an adult, left organized religion entirely to instead devote herself to social justice. At thirteen, I'd sent her to an international camp where she was first exposed to the concept of veganism, animal rights, and political activism. When I dropped her off, the last thing she asked for was Kentucky Fried Chicken. By the time I picked her up ten days later, she never ate chicken (or cheese or even honey) again.

There are other details to my story that might explain further why things happened the way they did, but that is not the point. I do not believe I am any more unique than my mother in having a loving relationship with a child who doesn't happen to see the world, or God, in precisely the same way that I do. And I am fairly confident that the world would be a happier place if we could all mindfully acknowledge that although we can "train a child up in the way he (or she) should go" it is not our job to manipulate them into reflections of ourselves.

Teens must be allowed and encouraged to explore. Regardless of their faith or reason-based worldview, the fact is many teens live by feelings—and that can result in lots of what Gandhi calls "the freedom to err." Teen mood swings fling back and forth like swings on a playground in the wind, which can make spiritual grounding feel only as great or as small as the latest triumph or tragedy. Reminding our teens that their emotions need not determine their ultimate mindset can protect their equilibrium.

I'll never forgot one of the most impactful lessons my mother taught me, when someone in my social circle didn't like me. She said, "Pam, what is the worst thing that can happen if she never does?" I was fourteen at the time, and I remember thinking about it a second and then bursting out laughing. Mom was right. It didn't matter unless I told myself it did. It wasn't a "religious" lesson, but in terms of real-life application of a spiritual principle (in this case, forgiveness), it was tops.

Why should spiritual training matter at all? The old adage says nature abhors a vacuum, and minus something to believe in human beings can become untethered and destabilized. Emotions can masquerade as "true," and an ego-based way of seeing the world can run rampant. When a teen places trust in something as subjective as feelings, they are on shaky ground. What if a boyfriend or girlfriend breaks up with them, or the family has to move to another state?

The confidence of that teen needs a strategy to remain firm, and that is where a spiritual understanding becomes critical. Whether through prayer, meditation, or simply communing with nature through a walk in the woods, they need tools to connect them to the bigger picture of their lives.

Tool 2: Spiritual Healing within a Toxic Culture

> *The fastest way to break the cycle of perfectionism and become a fearless mother is to give up the idea of doing it perfectly—indeed to embrace uncertainty and imperfection.*
>
> —Arianna Huffington

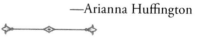

Perfectionism is the trap that keeps on trapping—its caustic impact destroys not only relationships and self-esteem, but projects and endeavors that collapse under the weight of needing to do it perfectly or not at all. Loving parents know how to teach their kids to "get over themselves" and do a "good enough job"

without chasing impossible aims. This has to begin with letting go of our own irrationally lofty goals.

We must also guard against allowing our teens to believe the tempting lies of a media/culture designed to tie their worth to objects, material possessions, and social status. Capitalism makes a lousy muse and an even worse compass. The road of greed and personal-gain-as-god leaves teen and adults both feeling depleted, dejected, and wondering if that's all there is. The good news is, by teaching our teens to anchor their purpose inside of themselves, they need never feel that alienation again.

What if their purpose is totally different than what our culture likes to say is "normal? What if their purpose is to evolve emotionally and spiritually, and our job is not to hinder that process? Can they forgive themselves and others? That is a skill it would be very helpful for them to have, don't you think? Can they learn to override any self-destructive inclinations or tendencies? Can their experience in doing so eventually inspire others?

What role might shame and feelings of unworthiness play in all of this spiritual independence? It's hard to stand on your own two feet when the enemy lies within one's own mind. Vulnerability is not a popular word in American culture, but it is actually a form of extreme courage and paradoxical strength. The truly great men and women throughout history have all been vulnerable at times, for without that they would hardly seem human. It is through the struggles, challenges, and missteps that we all eventually find our way "home." Perfection almost never precedes anything true or lasting. It is an illusion, or mass delusion, as toxic as any our culture germinates.

How's this for a "purpose": to live a happy life filled with kindness? Or this: for your teen to aspire to help those around him or her to live happier lives for themselves? Or this: to remember their own intrinsic value and the sacredness of their interconnection with all other beings on this planet? Or even this: to care for themselves with such tenacity and determination that they attract only the most like-minded of partners and associates in both their personal and professional lives?

Tool 3: Reminding Them of Context

I work really hard at trying to see the big picture and not getting stuck in ego. I believe we're all put on this planet for a purpose . . . when you connect with that love and that compassion, that's when everything unfolds.

—Ellen DeGeneres

Teens think in the snapshot; it's up to parents to help them frame the feature-length motion picture. Without the 30+ years of life experience parents have and often take for granted, each minor challenge a teenager faces can be perceived as a disaster. Teen suicide rates attest that they sometimes even take the most desperate measures possible as they seek a permanent solution to a temporary problem. One of the saddest events of my life was attending the funeral for a pretty, popular, fun-loving 14-year-old girl who lived in our community in Virginia. This bright student with her entire life ahead was emotionally undone when her boyfriend broke up with her. Devastated, she took a shotgun and killed herself on the front lawn.

Everybody hurts, so the song says. Everybody cries. Everybody also makes mistakes, and for teens this can feel devastating.

Shame can choke them and steal their joy as quickly as anything on earth. Helping them navigate their disappointments as well as celebrate their successes is so important for parents looking to strengthen the types of bonds that will bode well into their 20s and beyond. Spiritual principles like faith, hope, joy, charity, and, yes, forgiveness, are what parents need to ensure is transmitted to the teen. The vehicle within which those values arise is less important than their tangible presence in the choices the burgeoning young adult will make on a daily basis that impact the world around them.

Two loving parents and sisters, all of whom were active in a local church community, by the way, surrounded the lovely teenager who died that day. They graciously received those of us in attendance with our own teens as we came through the funeral line. Many of us were speechless with grief. Her parents had lovingly placed vivacious photos of their little girl—toddler, tween, and teen—alongside a soccer ball and letterman's jacket in a display around her casket. A long line of weeping high school students wove through the lobby of our local funeral home. Many of them still honor her in Facebook posts.

I will never get over the feeling of realizing that family could have been anyone's. There can be neither rhyme nor reason when tragedy of this magnitude strikes, but it should give parents pause to examine how we might even more mindfully equip our own teenage children.

Faith cannot be inherited. It is not contagious and cannot be "caught." Parents didn't do anything wrong if their children grow up with unique perspectives, and deserve no praise if the child happens to agree with them. Perhaps the parent of a prodigal did everything right by respecting the autonomy and individual relationship that young person has with whatever higher power rules the universe; perhaps the parent of a seemingly obedient "mini-me" child has actually inhibited the natural right of every individual on Earth to seek a personal, unique relationship to the world around them.

For parents with particular faith traditions, it is imperative to live out the faith as a 3-dimensional model—with actions, not merely words. Teens hear so many confusing messages about what they should do or should be. You know what they really "listen" to? The unspoken sermons contained within the cause and effect of the choices of significant adults and peers in their lives. Actions speak louder than words; each parent's life must be the lesson, whether one of example or warning.

Tool 4: Defining Their Purpose in Life

The purpose of life is not to be happy. It is to be useful, to be honorable, to be compassionate, to have it make some difference that you have lived and lived well.

—Ralph Waldo Emerson

Teens feel anxiety about everything from grades to chores to family matters to social pressures. Whether it's wearing the right Abercrombie outfit, being invited to the right party, attending prom with the right date, or simply figuring out a way not to be humiliated by a sibling attending the same school, life at 15 can feel like a puzzle missing a few pieces. That can really stink, especially when all you really want is to get your drivers license and carve out some breathing room for yourself . . . away from all that *pressure.*

Just visit your local bookstore—if you can still find one, that is—and you'll find a self-help section chock-full of books designed to help people of all types and descriptions "find their purpose." It's as if the human race has collectively decided that there is one specific goal each person should ascertain for himself or herself, and once finding it pursue in a linear and speedy fashion until they exhaust themselves.

New Year's resolutions rarely last beyond February, and yet people perpetually make them. Why is that? Maybe it's because many of us have a sinking feeling that we're missing out on something important. Projecting that onto our teenagers, though, is totally unfair. If parents aren't really sure how to articulate something as lofty as "our purpose in life," then how the heck can we expect a sophomore in high school to do it?

An unfortunate habit of many well-intentioned moms and dads is feigning knowing more than we do. We like to pretend to know things, to have answers, and to present edicts to our teens like kindly dictators who—truth be told—are just as confused as anybody about what the heck we're all doing here in this thing called life.

And here's the real trap—even when we find one purpose (parenting, for example, or starting a new business) we must juggle the incessant demands of each new incident and circumstance life hurls in our directions. Don't get me wrong, much of it is blissful, but few can argue the fact that purpose is less linear and more like a winding pathway.

Another complication comes when we encourage our teens (or ourselves) to see purpose as necessarily something tangible, achievable, and outside of ourselves. The cultural stews in which we all marinate seem to assume that there is a "there" there—as if there is one perfect destination for each of us, and that until we arrive at this static location of bliss and perfection we are somehow missing the mark. We must detoxify from that delusion, and let our teens off the hook at the same time we escape that false belief.

Parents do well to recognize the limitations of our own ability to steer the course of our children's lives—especially as they traverse the wide terrain from freshman year to graduation. Teens need to discover and nurture their authentic nature, while figuring out a way to accept and even love themselves. That's it. Everything else they might do, be, or accomplish is merely the fruit that needs to grow from the original tree of self-acceptance, knowledge, and love—whether it's passionate relationships, inspired goals, meaningful careers, or volunteer work. Those things, although necessities of life, do not comprise a purpose.

When teens know that their purpose isn't expected to be specific and crystallized at age 16, they can take a deep breath and do something truly inspired—live. As much as we'd like to, we cannot constantly intervene to protect our kids. There will be times they are misunderstood, unappreciated, or rejected. Sometimes others will value their work; sometimes they won't. They might give and give, but still get little or nothing in return. As parents, we must inoculate them against the need for others to give them value. They must learn to be self-generating people who appreciate themselves and others.

Tool 5: Fostering Patience through Hard Times

That which does not kill us makes us stronger.
—Friedrich Nietzsche

In this life, we all need to wear a helmet. It's a contact sport and not one of us gets out alive. With proper perspective, however, we might align ourselves and our children to the highest good possible in each of our lives. What if part of our purpose actually requires some measure of suffering? Can we "man up" (or "woman up") enough to move through it with grace? Can we remember that "this too shall pass" and allow the ebb and flow of life on life's terms to bring whatever wisdom this journey has in store for us?

There is an old saying that many teachers like to quote—"Experience is a hard teacher because she gives the test first, the lesson afterwards." This saying, credited to Vernon Saunders Law (a former science teacher and Major League Baseball athlete), is spot on. Our teens are going to have to fumble through their 20s just like most of us did, plain and simple. Even those who are fortunate enough to get pretty plaques with gold embossed seals from fancy universities on them will never find true worth or sense of purpose there. Sure, we hope they will love their work, and do it well. We pray that they will find a way to contribute to the human condition in some small or large way that perhaps alleviates suffering or at least doesn't perpetuate more of it.

We've all met or read about brilliant and effective celebrities, businesspeople, and superstars who glitter like gold on the outside, but are basically hollow inside—empty messes, often sour and sadly contagious since their veneer seems so seductive. We need to encourage our teens to aim for things that are real, that are lasting and true. So much in this world masquerades as real, but when we scratch the surface disappointment looms.

Let's not raise hollow people. This world needs the real deal, and that starts with vulnerability, wanders through self-forgiveness, and ends up someplace unforeseeable. Every saint has a past, and every sinner has a future. We're not perfect (at least, I know I'm not), and neither are our kids. But that doesn't mean we can't be great parents. A parent's love can be perfect, and perfect love trumps anything else that tries to stand against it. Just ask those moms lifting school buses off their kids. Are you surprised that their physical strength quadruples with adrenaline when their young are threatened? I'm not. Heaven help anyone who tries to harm the child of a parent who abides in perfect love.

Tool 6: Anchoring Them to the Present Moment

You don't live your life, but life lives you. Life is the dancer, and you are the dance.

—Eckhart Tolle

Eckhart Tolle encourages his millions of readers to live in the present moment—in the "now of the now." One interesting aspect of people being disingenuous is that they generally perpetuate these false versions of themselves in order to either mask where they've been, or anticipate and manipulate where they'd like to go. Shame of the past, and/or preference for a particular flavor of future, are intricately implicated as cause for the sad shadow boxing of the real self with the persona.

How can we as parents help our teens to summon the courage to rally their true selves, and to abide by their values and principles . . . come what may? It has to begin with acceptance. Just as the alcoholic must surrender any notion that he or she will ever be "normal" again, so each budding spiritual being must let go of the delusion that they are in control. Each teen must come to believe that sanity exists only in truthfulness, and each parent must jealously guard that honesty in their teen as they navigate the fragile passage from high school to life outside of the parent's home.

Loving parents recognize that the inside job of spiritual growth has little to do with rituals and buildings, with dogma and ceremony. Although certainly these activities can enrich lives, they do not in and of themselves constitute spirituality. I cannot tell you how many parents I've known over the years who thought they were doing their part in getting their children to youth group or a church service who later blanched to realize these rituals meant little to their children, and once they'd grown the rind was tossed aside to reveal the true pulp within.

We must ask ourselves, "Whose faith is this, anyway?" The trick with Tolle's work is to not think about it. Most people, the author says, are lost in thought. The suggestion to "be out of your mind" may sound bizarre, but he squarely advocates for moving from thought into experience. For example, what is happening, right here, right now? Where are you as you read this book? Can you observe the thinker—that part of your mind that is processing this information while perhaps sitting under a glorious tree or in the presence of a magnificent sunset?

When our teens are weaned to always think and analyze, they learn to argue and figure things out, but perhaps not to be blissfully present in the truest sense. Have you ever driven home and not really remembered much about how you got there? Often, we are lost in thought. No one gets anywhere trying to figure out a tree. If you try to analyze the beauty of a sunset, you find its magic cannot be weighed. To measure a tree requires you to cut it down to count the rings. Is this the way we want our teens to experience the world, as a series of facts, thoughts, data?

Or might there be more?

Are we afraid of the infinite possibilities for both good and evil that our children bring to the world around us? Just ask the mother of any convicted felon, and you'll have an answer. Our children can bring glory and honor to the family name and legacy, or shame and ridicule. The stakes can feel frighteningly high, which for some parents results in attempts to overly control their teen as they make choices. When natural inclinations toward autonomy and individuation appear in those teens, chaos ensues in the family dynamic.

Each child is a unique expression of the mixed DNA of two parents with some pixie dust sprinkled on top. We must courageously remind them not to shrink, even in a world that validates conformity. They must be encouraged to stay encouraged. Being brave doesn't mean they might not feel afraid when facing major obstacles and decisions in their lives, but they must know that we as their parents are standing by supporting them. When they are present in the moment, and fortified by loving adults who guide them appropriately, anything is possible.

Chapter 12

TYPES

We cannot fashion our children after our desires, we must have them and love them as God has given them to us.

—Johann Wolfgang Goethe

I'd like to take an opportunity to introduce you to 3 very specific types of students that I've encountered over my many years both as a teacher and a parent. As it turns out, I'm a mother of 3 children, with each of my daughters falling into one of 3 distinct categories. When I meet new students, I've come to fairly quickly identify each type, and have ended up giving them a name in my own mind to be sure I see them accurately (and therefore teach optimally): in my estimation, approximately 20% of teens are Type 1, 60% are Type 2, and 20% are Type 3.

In this chapter I offer a description of each of type of student—the particular benefits and challenges that each possesses, and most importantly some strategies for parents and educators in dealing with each type.

Type 1: Prodigals

Let's begin with Type 1—the Prodigals. As you may recall in the biblical story of the Prodigal Son in Luke chapter 15, he wanders away from the father and squanders his inheritance on women, wine, and fast living. This irritates the other sibling in the family, especially when the Prodigal Son comes back to the father after having wasted everything that he had been given.

The Prodigal comes back home in desperation, saying, "Please, may I just have the crusts of food and the garbage that you are feeding to the pigs out in the back of the home? For although I am not worthy to be called your son anymore, I am starving and may die without your mercy." In the story, the father lovingly wraps his arms around his wayward son and says, "Let us kill the fatted calf and throw a celebration, for my son was lost and now he is found." Sibling rivalry being what it is, you can imagine how the obedient brother responds.

Interestingly, this parallels what happens for students in a school system when their nature is somewhat rebellious or defiant. In the Diagnostic and Statistical Manual of Mental Disorders (DSM IV) manual used in the field of psychology, there is actually a diagnosis called ODD—Oppositional Defiant Disorder. It almost makes me smile when I think about this label being put on teenagers, because if you've ever raised one you know that, depending on which way the wind is blowing and the mood of your child on a particular day, many if not most teens seem diagnosable. Almost all have days where one could say, "We should have this teen tested for ODD, they're being very oppositional, and also quite defiant."

So, is this a diagnosable disorder? Well, of course it is in some cases. Without minimizing that, here the discussion is students who, as Prodigals, march to their own drummers. The Type 1 understands that they're in a school system that is demanding their conformity, and are either irritated or amused by that fact. There are several different types.

I've seen students who absolutely have that little smirk on their face as they sit the back of the classroom. Very often, unfortunately, these are students who end up falling out of the school system entirely—dropping out at 14, 15, or 16. Becoming so disenchanted with what they perceive as a false system, they truly just check out mentally, intellectually, and eventually physically from the entire endeavor.

There are other students that I have seen, also Type 1, who are more amused by it. These are sometimes the class clowns, sometimes those who show up but are not taking it too seriously because they have x-ray vision to see through the ruse of the entire educational system. I have to give these students credit by the way, because I would have to agree that the proverbial emperor is sometimes wearing no clothes. There is sort of a gallows humor to realizing that you're in a system with presumed authority and that knowledge is being passed down from this supposedly superior person to you as their hypothetical inferior. In fact, I would argue that excellent teaching allows for a meeting of mutual minds, with wisdom as a mutual exchange.

Type 1 students are challenging to get through a traditional educational system. Many end up being homeschooled because their parents don't know what else to do with them. A fair percentage ends up in boarding schools or other live-in situations.

I have known Type 1 students who were shipped off to wilderness camps or military schools. It's understandable when conservative parents sometimes experience panic or at the very least concern when their student is so far afield from their own values.

Here is my experience: my firstborn daughter is what I consider to be a Prodigal. Very intelligent, she nonetheless loathed her school years because her DNA is wound around nonconformity. In fact, her earliest academic experience was a terrific Catholic school in New York City located on Fifth Avenue. This was a very elite school populated by the children of celebrities and New York power couples. By 3rd grade the nuns approached me and said, "Your daughter is inciting rebellion among her friends on the playground. They don't want to listen to the teacher. They've all decided to be pirates and Pink Ladies from *Grease*! We've decided, based on this and some other behaviors that we are seeing in the classroom, that maybe our school isn't the proper fit for her."

When she came home that day I didn't know what to say. In fact it was many years later before I had told her what actually happened. I didn't want her to feel rejected. I knew that indeed she marched to her own drummer, and had a lot of charisma and persuasiveness. I had little doubt all those sweet little girls in their sweet little uniforms were doing things they weren't supposed to be doing because my precious firstborn daughter had somehow led a mutiny on the bountiful Upper East Side.

I will never forget her coming home at 8 years of age, taking a Sharpie from my desk to her little pale blue pinafore uniform, and writing all over it as an artistic expression, "I am not a robot, I am not a robot." She decided to be happy to be leaving that school because she was very frustrated with the teachers and administration, but of course she would miss her fellow Pink Ladies and pirates dearly. She came up to me in the kitchen from our brownstone basement with a little Prodigal grin on her face. Her fingers were all Sharpie-black. I said, "Sweetie, go wash your hands; it's almost time for dinner." There you go—that's my earliest personal experience with a Type 1.

I can tell you if you fast forward, the teen years were bumpy; she will be the first to tell you that. Thankfully, though, when the time came we did find a college and a major that she loved. After she graduated at the top of her class with a degree in Psychology and her minor in Women's Studies, she went on to make her career working with autistic children and the rescue of animals that have been neglected or abandoned. She is a born leader, and that was evident even on the playgrounds of Central Park when she was in 3rd grade. In hindsight, it all makes perfect sense.

She now works with several national nonprofit organizations. One raises hundreds of thousands of dollars annually for local charities by auctioning off signed guitars by classic rock stars as they tour across the country. She also works with a major national wildlife conservation nonprofit organization, advocating for the humane treatment of big cats and other animals. Finally, each summer she volunteers with a camp for young tween and teenage girls teaching self-empowerment through music, the arts, and personal growth. She still likes to inspire a rebellion or two, but now that revolves around raising people's consciousness about gender inequities in American culture, minimizing cruelty to animals, and voicing her own unique political views. She has done tremendous work in both the nonprofit and academic sectors, and is a successful (still non-conforming) young woman in her twenties now.

Allow me to speak a word of encouragement to the moms and dads out there: you've just got to raise them with an unusual level of patience and understanding. The more pressure you lay on a

Type 1 to conform, the more they're going to push back at you. Not that they are ODD, but they are wired in a certain way that they need to be given options and a sense of autonomy, making decisions, and being heard. Being allowed to be who they are, having a sense of authenticity? Very important to the Type 1.

Another Type 1 I taught several years ago was a female student who was already in her late teens and had not made it through tenth grade. She came and sat in on a 9th grade class that I was teaching on *Romeo and Juliet*. She was going through her Goth phase with the rudimentary dark makeup and ripped black clothes to match the scowl on her face. She plopped down in the back of the room and looked at me like, "Who's this lady; what in the world can she possibly teach *me*?" Well.

Fast forward 6 weeks later. We had finished the play. She came up to me after class and said, "You know, Ms. D.," and she was from Australia so she had this wonderful accent, "I decided I'm going to go ahead and take the test even though I'm not going to get credit for this year because I cut school too much. But I'm going to go ahead and take the test because I actually kind of like this sh*t and I want to see how I do." She took the test and passed it with an 88/B+ (and my tests are not easy). She was so proud of that she said, "I took it to me mum and dad and they wanted to frame it on the fridge." It was evidence that she's capable of greatness; she's just someone who has to be approached in the right way.

Perhaps having raised a Type 1 helped me know how to handle a situation like that. The following summer this Australian student "friended" me on Facebook long after I was no longer her teacher. I have since become a private mentor of sorts for her. She is now a successful actor and songwriter—with a mounting resume of national roles as well as considerable musical ability. She is developing lyrics that express her own true voice, and I applaud her for that. She even accompanied my two younger daughters and me to the beach in Santa Monica one day. We had a wonderful time and took lots of pictures. She recently posted a new red carpet photo on Facebook. She was wearing a green velvet dress, heels, flawless natural makeup— and zero evidence of that angry Goth girl I'd met a few years earlier. Isn't it funny? A Type 1 is just someone waiting to be seen and heard for who they are. When they get that, they can really surprise people.

Type 2: Proficients

Many more students are Type 2 in the bell curve of our educational system than the other two combined. These are the Proficients, who seem to be wired in way that allows them to successfully navigate the current structures and systems we call "school." I estimate about 60% of the population falls into this category, so it's an important category to look at.

Certainly in terms of academic excellence and competence, there are going to be all shades of grey along that bell curve. Some will be the straight-A students, many will not. Maybe they struggle in a subject or two, but by and large students who are Type 2 are academically advantaged because they are hard wired to be willing to conform. They may not necessarily love it, but they are constitutionally capable of it.

It is my experience that it's not the parents who create that, by the way. I believe children just . . . arrive. Otherwise, how can I explain as a mother why I have each of these types of students in my family? How do you explain that? They are getting the same DNA, but the way that the genes mix and mingle is a dance all its own. Certainly nature and nurture each play a role.

Type 2s are willing to conform; therefore, in the school environment the greatest challenge for this category of students is in helping them find the authenticity that the Type 1 teens already have in spades. In fact if we could take the compliance and the willingness of the Type 2s and give some of that to the Type 1s, and then give some steely Type 1 authenticity and determination to the Type 2s, both groups would benefit.

Type 2 students very often, by the time they get to the 10th and 11th grade, are lost in determining who to become or how to cast a vision for their future lives. They are so used to conforming that they actually aren't sure who they are. They want to look to the adults in their lives for answers. "Well, my dad was a doctor, so maybe I should be a doctor," they think. Or, "Well, my guidance counselor thinks I'd make a great lawyer, so maybe I should do that."

Rather than having that internal drive that we sometimes see in other types of students, very often Type 2s are encumbered by the very conformist inclinations the American education system has evolved to encourage and even require. This group requires guidance and support. I especially encourage parents of Type 2s to seek the mentors outside the family I described earlier in this book. Seek scoutmasters, counselors, friends from church, teachers/tutors, and neighbors. At least two or three mentors who are not their parents and not relatives need to be in the lives of these students to begin helping them build a vision for who they are in the world separate from the parent. They are going to have to individuate as they travel across those teenage years, and it's sometimes difficult for them to fully do so.

My second daughter is a Type 2. She has generally been an A and B student. Every once in a while she will get a lower grade in a subject, but she typically pulls herself back up when she applies herself. She doesn't have any learning differences, is not particularly rebellious, and enjoys a lot of social popularity. Still, she struggles to identify who she is and wants to become. One thing we began doing around third grade was getting her involved in music as a form of expression.

Playing piano has become an important outlet for her. Having played for many years now, music has become a way for her to find and express her "voice." She speaks not just through words, but also through her fingers on the keyboard. It probably won't surprise you to hear that her piano teacher has become one of her primary mentors. She is a wonderful professional musician here in Los Angeles, a very cool cat—late twenties, always dressed in some funky outfit, a smile on her face, super energetic, passionate about her subject, knows music theory, and teaches it well.

In fact, this mentor picks my daughter up from school one day a week. They chat in the car. My daughter talks about what's happening at school or what happened at a recent party among her friends. Her teacher is someone who has earned a place as a trusted advisor in her life, and I'm delighted that she has her to go to. In fact, recently her father gave her an acoustic guitar for her 14th birthday, and most nights I can hear her working out the chords for Pink Floyd and Green Day songs down the hall. Pretty awesome, and it beats the heck out of her getting high or running away to deal with the stress that naturally accompanies this stage in life.

Like my second daughter, I see myself as falling into this category. Both she and I have experienced issues related to our physical voices, and I see this as possibly related to what I am describing here. In my case, the physical manifestation of problems with my voice required surgery on my vocal chords at age eleven. I am now convinced it was partially psychologically induced. In terms of my physical health, which is hearty and strong, my voice has proven my one Achilles' heel. Finding my voice as a writer and teacher has probably saved my life.

Think about the Disney Princesses. Where are they? They are sitting in castles, not necessarily empowered with anything resembling a voice. In fact, one of the most popular princess stories—Ariel, the little mermaid—voluntarily exchanges her right to be heard so she can become part of a man's world. You do the math on how this might subliminally affect generations of girls as they come of age. Poor unfortunate souls indeed if they try to navigate this world voiceless. I thank God that I found mine, and I'd rather lose any other ability I possess than the ability to speak with conviction. Interestingly, my daughter in this category has chosen child psychology as her intended major in college. She wants to help others find their voices, too.

Type 3: Pearls

Our final category, Type 3, is very near and dear to my heart. These are the Pearls. My definition of a Type 3 student is one who is "non-neurotypical," usually falling into one of two categories. The first is the gifted population, academically testing in the top 3 to 5% among their same-aged peers. The second group of has diagnosable learning differences. Some have ADHD, dyslexia, visual or cognitive processing issues, or dwell somewhere along the spectrum for autism.

Type 3s are unique creatures within the educational system, as each is able to teach the teacher things that the teacher does not yet know. (Of course, I'd argue this is true for all students anyway, but there is still something uniquely special about these students.) It's important when working with them to honor the fact that they are not just going to be able to hammer through a curriculum. They require enrichment or remediation, and at either end of the gamut they thrive with teachers who are adroit with spontaneous modifications based upon real-time exchanges. They are anything but one-size-fits-all, and strictly regimented lesson plans rarely serve them.

Like Type 1s, who occasionally skip school and then decide to show up when they feel like it, you cannot plow through a set of material with Type 3s because they know that they are exceptional. By exceptional I don't mean better or worse, but most know intuitively that they are an exception to the rule. They are in a separate population, if you will, of the student body. Many students do have IEPs, or Individualized Education Plans, to help them implement the curricula in their schools. I have worked in both public and private schools over the years, and participated in many IEP meetings. Key teachers meet with the school psychologist, the parents and sometimes with the student to discuss how to modify or approach class work given the fact that they do have these learning differences.

Like those Type 3s with IEP support, the gifted and talented students also require additional services in traditional school settings. These high functioning students become easily bored without enrichment, time with peers, and innovative/expansive opportunities with a driven educator experienced in serving the needs of their population. Without gifted and talented pull out groups, these students get fidgety with the slow pace of regular classrooms, which by definition must cater to the "norm" and not the exception.

Sadly, many public schools fail to provide such services, or when they do so, it is without fully integrating what the students need in order to maintain the status quo. It sometimes seems as if they are being encouraged to play down their own excellence in order to keep the peace. Teachers sometimes feel threatened by what they perceive as an uppity student, even if those young people are on the precipice of some wonderful theoretical or creative breakthrough.

These gifted Type 3s need to be in pullout situations at least once or twice a week, where they are with students that can keep up with them, otherwise they are going to be bored out of their minds. Ideally, they will be homeschooled or placed in special private school setting that caters to other kids like them. Quite honestly, only a small percentage of most teachers can keep up with some of these students. Imagine a teen who is already extremely brilliant being in a classroom with a teacher who is perhaps less insightful than they are.

Of course most teachers are very intelligent, and many have master's degrees, but that doesn't make them ideal instructors for gifted students. If teachers themselves follow the 20-60-20 proportions I estimate, then the odds are most of them are not a categorical match.

On the IEP-supported student side, equal expertise needs to come into play on the part of the educator, and unfortunately many have neither the training nor the patience required to be able to mesh well with this part of the population. What used to be called "Special Ed students" are now called "students with learning differences." The politically correct shift in language notwithstanding, stigmas can still abound.

Thankfully, trends have allowed this population to largely be mainstreamed into regular classrooms. This means that out of 25 or 30 students in a room, a set proportion, usually not more than 20 to 25% of the room (depending on the school's policies) is comprised of students with learning differences mixed in with regular education students. Very often a secondary teacher assists in these rooms. Although it's not explicitly stated, it's usually a Special Education teacher who is primarily keeping an eye on the students who are in that population. They ensure IEP students navigate that class's requirements appropriately, when properly placed and trained.

My youngest daughter was diagnosed with learning differences when she was ten years old. Multiple doctors at UCLA Medical Center concurred, and her father and I were relieved to have a label even though it was frustrating to not have known that sooner. Although through her younger years we realized there were differences, we never understood what they were. We knew she had trouble focusing, and some social difficulties, but without a clear understanding of how her thinking worked, we were at a loss to help her.

Her diagnosis empowered me to be able to talk to her teachers, and guided all the adults in her life to be aware of shifting the way we addressed her academic needs. Fast forward to where she is today. This stalwart Type 3, who has endured so much and come so far, is holding a solid B average in school. She is in a mainstream classroom, with the additional support a couple of afternoons a week with a Special Education specialist, a wonderful woman whom she also considers a friend and mentor.

This daughter has taken and enjoyed dance classes, which helps her to physicalize some of her frustrations; expressing herself through dance has increased her self-esteem exponentially even though she is self-conscious about not matching some of the other girls in her body type. I am proud of her for loving herself as the strong, beautiful girl she is, even though some unkind peers have teased and even bullied her.

If you've ever parented a child who has been bullied, you probably know like I do some of the most searing kind of pain imaginable. Sometimes you just want to move to a cabin in the woods to protect them from the unkindness of strangers. I almost hesitated to even share this here, because I so want to protect my beautiful daughter. However, I know that bullying is rampant in our society, and believe it would be dishonest and unfair of me not to include the truth. I have taught her to hold her head up, to defend herself when necessary, and to speak up to her teachers and me if it doesn't stop. She is making progress socially, and I am proud of her courage.

She also played on a volleyball team this past year. She is very tall for her age so guess what? This pearl of a girl can spike the ball. Being 5'10" at twelve years old has its advantages. What a wonderful application of her unique gifts and way for her to be able to express herself as the awesome Type 3 that she is. She is also a very talented visual artist, loves anime, and has recently taken to learning all about cosmetology. Her current life goal is to begin a line of cosmetics. She is very good at applying makeup to herself and to others, and would live in upscale beauty stores if they'd allow it.

She teaches and inspires me, and the others around her, to appreciate the uniqueness that she brings. All Type 3s do this. They cause us to marvel, and teach us to recognize the value of the exceptional person that is in front of us. Like others, Pearls cannot be seen as a mere number or chalk outline called "student," but demand and deserve unique consideration.

I hope that these three categories have created helpful ways of thinking about the students that you have in your life. If you are a teacher or parent figure, I encourage you to consider the students that you have taught over the years. Each of us could easily start making a mental list of our own families of origin and children we've brought into the world. I grew up in a family of three, and we were well distributed among the three types just like my daughters are—I had a Type 3 brother and a Type 1 sister, as I navigated the path of the Type 2. Then again, I have known families with four Type 1 brothers, so there are no patterns to rely upon.

Think of your brothers and sisters, your children, your nieces and nephews, and your students: which are Type 1? Type 2? Type 3? Sometimes knowing *whom* you're teaching can help you know *how* to teach them.

Checklist #4

FOR SPIRITUAL INDEPENDENCE

🔒 Be mindful to set an example of living, not just speaking, your own faith and beliefs, if you have them. Teens hate hypocrisy even more than adults, and they sniff it out like a beagle on hunt day.

🔒 Expose your child to various perspectives and alternate worldviews in addition to your own.

🔒 Encourage respect for the spiritual paths of all peoples.

🔒 Take personal inventory of your levels on honesty in your relationship with your teenager, and consider using the Twelve Steps to help you increase intimacy through deeper truth and connection.

🔒 Offer freedom to explore and embrace an individual view of the world and of "faith"—whatever that means to them. No one ever got to heaven on Grandma's skirt tail anyway.

🔒 Offer antidotes for toxic aspects of our culture, and notice when they need to plug back in to nature.

- 🛈 Help them find context—seeing the big picture will position them for future stability.
- 🛈 Foster patience—with them and in them.
- 🛈 Guide them toward a sense of purpose for school and the other things they "do"—what is the "why?"

SEND YOUR STUDENT TO COLLEGE WITHOUT GOING BROKE

Sam Mikhail

A note about the contributing author: Sam Mikhail, founder of College Made Easy, a nationally acclaimed academic and college planning firm based in Southern California, has saved his clients tens of millions of dollars off the cost of college.

I f the insanely high cost of putting your kids through college has you a little freaked out, believe me, I understand. After all, even a "normal" college education can cost $75,000 to $200,000. That's a heck of a lot of money. I mean, when I think about how baby boomers who attended in the 1970s and 1980s, applied to 2 or 3 colleges, were accepted to 2 or 3 colleges, and spent only a couple grand a year, it truly does seem like ancient history.

Every fall, millions of students enter college and leave a wake of mistakes, because nobody really told them what they needed to do. Even though the process has changed many times over the years, competition has increased 10-fold, and college costs have skyrocketed; most folks that are actually planning like it's still 1980—the old fashioned way. In 2012, more than 50% of entering students are forecast to drop out before they graduate. If they only knew a few simple truths, they could save themselves a lot of grief and money. Well, I've got great news for you.

You don't want your child saddled with $50,000 to $250,000 of crippling debt from student loans—and you don't want him or her to be forced to work a minimum wage job while trying to study at all hours of the night.

Some colleges' financial aid officers might prefer I didn't provide you with this information, because they don't like their well-kept secrets being revealed to you. Parents are left in the dark about much of the process.

We haven't met yet, but we already know a lot about each other. I know you're probably a parent of a college-bound high school student, and you are wondering how in the world you can afford to send your child to a decent college these days. Naturally, you want to give him or her the best chance in life, but you also are concerned, because you can't work forever. You're wondering whether after paying for college you'll have enough to pay your mortgage payment. How about your living expenses? Funding your retirement?

You want the best education possible for your child. You already know that the right college or university can set your child up for a lifetime of success. You have most likely been overcome by panic at the fear that, especially in this economy, you don't know how you are going to comfortably pay for that education.

Here are the most common mistakes parents make:

1. Starting Too Late

Things will come to those who wait—but only what is left over from those who hustle. Most high school students and parents start to really think about college late in their junior or early in their senior year. This is fine if you are going to a local community college, but not if you want to go to a college or university. The best time to start preparing for college is NOW. I consistently get asked, "When is the best time to start planning?" I recommend beginning to plan for college at the end of 8th or beginning of 9th grade, if possible. Why, you may ask? Because the two most important high school years for colleges are the sophomore and junior years. Students have to be ready in advance to perform at their highest level. When they are a senior or even a junior for that matter, they can't go back in time and fix mistakes made the year or two before. There is a lot of work that needs to be done. Don't delay.

2. Relying on Your High School Counselor

Many public and private high school counselors understand the need for a qualified full-service college planner who can help build the proper college list, while making college affordable for the family. Most school counselors don't have time to pilot students through a college prep process. They can give some passing advice, but no real one-on-one strategic coaching. Also understand that high school counselors are not college counselors; they are high school counselors, and their job is to get you through high school, not necessarily through college. There are some very good guidance and college counselors, but most of them don't have time, resources or knowledge to do a thorough job on college prep, even at the best private schools.

There are some questions you need to ask. Can your high school counselor really help you:

1. Increase the amount of gift-aid from colleges by assessing the historical gift-aid trends for a particular student's profile?

2. Advise on your financial profile so that your student can legally qualify for more federal, state and other grant money?

3. Fill out all the financial aid forms for you, accurately and on time?

4. Pick colleges that grant more gift-aid?

3. Taking the SAT or ACT Too Late

The majority of parents tell me that they were advised to have their student take the SAT or ACT late in their junior year or perhaps even early in their senior year. It is very frustrating to see the amount of destructive information being recycled to unwitting parents each year. I also see too many students take their first test without any proper test preparation. When a senior takes a SAT/ACT test for the first time, there is no time to train or improve those results. They have only one chance before it's too late. These parents/students are often cornered into a desperate situation, and have to settle on what they can get in college choices and whatever funds they can scrape up. Start taking the tests early, and prepare properly. By working with the caliber of tutors associated with a company like Valley Prep Tutoring in Los Angeles, whether in person or via Skype, the possible 200 to 400 points on the SAT (2 to 4 points on the ACT) may mean higher admissions rates. All tutors are not created equal, and top-of-the-line support makes an important difference.

4. Thinking Grades Aren't Good Enough

Some parents think whatever their child's grades may be, it's not enough to get them any gift aid, anywhere. Others think that no matter how low their child's grades are, somehow they have a chance to attend the college of their dreams, regardless of how out-of-reach it may be. The truth is, there is a college for every student. Most competitive, college-bound students have a non-weighted (meaning out of a 4.0 scale maximum) GPA between 3.3 and 4.0. What I see many parents/students do is build an imbalanced and ineffective college list. This will reduce the number of colleges at which they have a chance of being accepted. Properly matching and balancing your child's college list can reduce college costs tremendously. Improving academic performance is another area in which we recommend making sure you have the right support and/or tutors.

5. Not Taking a College Prep Track

Just because you are in high school doesn't mean you are taking anything to prepare you for college. Most schools have an AP program, and some actually have SAT and ACT prep programs, but few have real college preparation processes. It's one thing to be enrolled in AP and Honors courses; it's another to use these classes to position your child properly. I've seen countless 3.3 GPA students (or even lower) who would have been 3.8 GPA students, if they had just a little guidance in properly building their class load. Many of these students even came from top private high schools. Their parents spend $10,000 to $50,000 a year to send their child to a great private high school, only to find that few colleges will accept their student after graduation. Students need to learn college success skills and few schools provide these, so they need to look outside for help.

6. Getting Bad Advice from Good People

Generally, friends and family want to help, and give advice on certain topics. They may have sent their child to college recently and may even have received a full ride. Some of the college process is pretty easy, and some of it is very complicated. Even students currently attending college are not experts—no more than getting your teeth cleaned by a dental hygienist qualifies you to perform a root canals. This is also true for parents who finished college 20+ years ago. Things are different now. Doctors give medical advice, lawyers give legal advice, so your best advice is from someone who has a record of success. There is too much future at stake and money at risk to leave this in the wrong hands.

7. Thinking College Is the Same As It Was When the Parents Went To College

To follow up on the previous section, parents often reflect on their own college experience, and get angry that the college process isn't like it was 10, 20, or 30 years ago. Well, we didn't have satellite TV, PCs, or the Internet when they went to college, so things are different, and thankfully so, in some ways. Today's college process and experience is different in every way as compared to even 5 years ago. For example, the University of California-Santa Barbara had a reputation for decades as being a party school. Well, the party is over, because a student now needs to have a minimum

3.70 non-weighted academic GPA to even have a chance of being accepted there. This is the case for many colleges.

8. Using a "Scholarship Service"

Beware! This is one of the biggest scams out there—each year tens of thousands of parents spend millions of dollars chasing elusive scholarships. Many websites will charge you, and even guarantee you a private scholarship. You don't need some expensive search program; the best place to get financial aid is from the college itself. I don't recommend spending a lot of time chasing outside scholarships unless they are really low hanging fruit. If you are determined to go after private scholarships, try to find ones that gift based upon something unique about your student. That way, you narrow down the pool of candidates from which the scholarship committee will choose.

When should you start getting help? Now. As you assemble the right team of professionals to support this important rite of passage, you will make sure your son or daughter has the best possible future.

Conclusion

EUPHORIA

Endorphins. Oh yeah.

Heading off for university is the final frontier for many teens. What no one warned me about was how I would feel when the day finally came to bring that little baby whom I'd so carefully guarded and raised for 17+ years to her new school. I will never forget the bittersweet feeling of moving my daughter into her first dorm. After the Costco run for supplies, the load-in of color-coordinated room accessories, I did something I didn't see coming. I cried. In fact, I cried most of the 45-minute drive back to our home. It was a mini-breakdown I suppose—the years of her life flashing in front of my eyes out of sequence as I tried to wrap my mind around the fact that she would never live in my home again.

Turns out I was right—she never did. Those were not tears of sadness; they were tears of joy. I had done it. I had run with perseverance the race marked out for me. I was—for lack of a better word—high on the feeling. I hadn't done it perfectly—far from it. But my daughter's ability to create a meaningful life for herself meant I'd done my job. I can only imagine many parents must feel the same way. Endorphins are powerful things, whether physical or emotional.

Nothing in this world I have ever done or will ever do compares to the stakes of parenthood. In my opinion, there is no greater accomplishment possible than in raising excellent human beings to move this tottering world forward along its evolutionary curve.

Addendum 1

IS COLLEGE NECESSARY
FOR SUCCESS TODAY?

Do students today need a college degree to become financially independent? Ask Mark Zuckerberg. The stark reality is that perusing a list of the top money-earners throughout American history, innovators abound who never crossed a threshold into college. Think Andrew Carnegie, Henry Ford . . . even Walt Disney.

In this Internet-centric, millennial generation, continuing changes in education, lifestyle, and the job market require parents to truly evaluate the actual realities of the job market before they plunk down $100,000 to send their sons and daughters to college. Not all degrees make money. Traditionally schools have hammered the concept that getting good grades and graduating from reputable schools is somehow a tacit ticket to success. With the advent of modern technology, however, this concept is almost obsolete. Although it is true to some extent, the debt from student loans should not eclipse the amount someone will earn from the job they will manage to get after graduation. Let's take a look at the cost-benefit analysis for a moment.

First, some bad news: the relative price tag of your high school student's completed college degree has skyrocketed in reverse proportion to probable career revenue. Happily, by implementing the following strategies toward your student's particular goals, success remains within reach. College need not be irrelevant, as long as the cost-benefit analysis is carefully considered before your student tosses his or her mortarboard hat in the air and you sign off on a costly acceptance package. As the parent of a college-bound teen, you need to seriously assess against the potential revenues your student's attainment of any particular degree will generate. This article will give you the data you need to make wise decisions.

According to the College Board, parents nowadays can plan to rack up quite a price tag—with tuition and fees plus room and board costing a staggering $20,000 (public) to more than $35,000 (private) on average. That is *per year*. Even with gift aid, merit aid, and scholarships, the numbers are often alarming. And before you multiply by four to calculate actual cost of attendance, factor in this little curve ball: more and more students are taking five or more years to graduate. *US News and World Report* data showed only 41 percent of students in 2010 made it in and out within a four-year cycle, and that number has declined every year since. Why? Economic trends now require many students to hold jobs while completing coursework. Meanwhile colleges are reducing classes offered to balance their budgets as incoming revenues decline. That means not every class needed for every degree can be realistically completed within four years.

Here's a non-rhetorical question: exactly how many graduates with communication majors will the job market be able to absorb in four to five years? We are often asking our teens the wrong questions. Parents ask, "What do you want to be when you grow up?" Perhaps they should reframe that: "What careers currently in demand do you feel you have an interest in doing? Which require skills or abilities that come naturally for you?" Let's acknowledge the fantasy of college-as-panacea. Many young people long to be a rapper, a pop star, an NFL linebacker, or a ballerina. Sidestepping college feels justifiable, but if those aspirations aren't quickly met, it can be a cold awakening. Some of the most talented screenwriters in Los Angeles tend bar.

The current marketplace rewards some majors and undervalues others, with economic success often falling to students graduating from top schools with degrees in science, business, or technology. There we see a much clearer career path with actual jobs forecast than in what I call waning majors.

According to *Forbes* magazine, the number-one worst choice of college major in economic terms is anthropology or archeology. Recent college graduates of the major, those ages twenty-two to twenty-six, can anticipate an unemployment rate over 10 percent, well above the national average. If they're lucky enough to land a job, the median salary is a paltry $28,000, compared to a mechanical engineer's initial wages of $58,000.

With low demand and low earnings, the arts and humanities are sadly also considered poor bets. Film, video, and photographic arts (number two) features a 12.9 percent unemployment rate for recent grads; fine arts (number three) has a rate of 12.6 percent; and philosophy and religious studies is a high 10.8%. All earn a median of just $30,000. Does this mean that your burgeoning actor should be dissuaded from studying theatre? No, but unless you expect them to be fortunate enough to become a major film star, be sure they can exercise that awesome creativity in revenue-producing ways as well to supplement their artistic endeavors if needed.

The high-priced attainment of low-demand degrees today has become the bane of millions of American college graduates who labor hard just to find jobs after they graduate. Do you want your sons and daughters to be one of the many struggling under nearly $30,000 in student loans attached to their names and social security numbers? Urge them toward practical applications of their skills and talents in their college educations, and avoid economic and logistic nightmares down the road.

Let's keep in mind, too, that a college degree is not always the key to success in life. Many college graduates today work in jobs that are not even remotely related to the degrees they've attained. Even graduates with business management degrees are not guaranteed to find careers in management-related fields unless they possess a wide variety of attributes, from the right networking skills and emotional intelligence to being a strong interviewee.

College should not be viewed as a path to become rich, but a vehicle to discovering one's true calling. Most college degrees are limited, in that they were designed to produce employees who will work for money instead of developing employers who generate money. Reading through the biographies of the wealthy shows they are usually successful investors and business owners, and by most counts more than half of them did not graduate from college.

Recent mega-success stories verify that at least some college can truly impact the right mind: Steve Jobs credits a course he took at Reed College before dropping out with inspiring Apple's aesthetics and branding, and Mark Zuckerberg's fledgling idea for Facebook tested its business model, target audience, and initial interface during his incomplete stint at Harvard. The $24.5

billion these two "college dropouts" have been able to generate speaks volumes about a new era of collegiate application.

Financial education is equally as powerful as a college degree. Entrepreneurial studies at schools like Babson and others are hot ticket items in the collegiate scene, and for good reason. More often than not, the media hype about graduating from college, getting a job, and automatically becoming successful is a fantasy for many parents seeking the right answers to unlock their students' futures. Wise parents remember to consider the particular skills and talents of their students, accurately assess the marketplace into which those attributes will be flung, and strategize accordingly.

The introduction of the Internet has opened a lot of opportunities for those willing to explore their options of attaining success beyond higher education. Imagine Emerson with an iPhone—things we take for granted as ordinary aspects of life today were unthinkable then. Now that the Industrial Age has given way and computer innovations have crept into nearly every conceivable sector of American commerce, financial success is facilitated more and more by innovation. To those who are willing to explore new avenues will flow the spoils in this brave new world. Success both on and off college campuses is now redefined by what it takes to monetize one's abilities, and the ability to create and innovate will lead the way.

Addendum 2
EDUCATIONAL REFORM

What is the purpose of an education? It seems such a basic question that no one thinks to ask it, but I'm willing to bet you'd agree that it's not just the answers in life that matter—it is knowing which questions to ask.

For me, the very word "school" conjures ambivalence regarding the world of institutionalized education. From the mania of parents prodding their youngsters to compete for academic accolades, to counter-cultural references in rock music, there can be little doubt that Western culture is anything but neutral on the topic of school. From Alice Cooper's "School's Out" ringing through the mid-June hallways of high schools, to the perennial popularity of Pink Floyd's menacing anti-school anthem "Another Brick in the Wall," we feel the backlash of students who have had it with the presumed authority of schools that not only often fail to educate them, but also fail to see them, accept them, or even emotionally, psychologically, intellectually, or physically protect them.

"If you don't eat your meat, you can't have any pudding!" shouts the menacing schoolmaster in the Pink Floyd song. If every teacher were a bombastic idiot like that, what parent could blame his or her teen for wanting to jump off the demented conveyer belt of a conformist school system?

Of course, all teachers don't scream imperatives at innocent students. We don't need no double negatives, but we also don't need no false demigods in fake chapels asking us to genuflect before altars of stone and ego. The issue is not the individuals. The issue is the system itself. Who the heck installed these conveyer belts in our students' lives? And how many moms and dads will it take to dismantle them, turn them into something useful, and point our children in the directions of each one's unique path in life?

What Pink Floyd's album and film *The Wall* demonstrated so accurately was the human need to connect, and to be seen. It echoes that other rock opera, The Who's *Tommy*, where the boy is disconnected from truth by damaged adults, and ends up dancing with Tina Turner as the acid queen. Pinball wizards and drug-addicted rock stars aside, the current age of technology and the post-millennial secondary educational system in America have brought our society to its knees.

According to Merriam-Webster's dictionary, the word "indoctrinate" dates back to 1626. This verb is defined as "to imbue with a usually partisan or sectarian opinion, point of view, or principle," and is derived from the Middle English *endoctrinen* and Anglo-French's *endoctriner*, from *en-* + *doctrine*. The word "doctrine" has a slightly less tainted connotation, but the word "indoctrinate" carries with it all the controlling negativity that a pedagogue might love. To indoctrinate is, in essence, the opposite of to educate—especially if you follow the adage about education necessitating the lighting of a fire rather than a filling of a bucket.

Pedagogues hate conflagration. Fire frightens them, and water feels much more soothing and quantifiable. The following lines from Robert Frost's poem "Fire and Ice" strike me as relevant:

Some say the world will end in fire,
Some say in ice.
From what I've tasted of desire
I hold with those who favor fire.
But if it had to perish twice,
I think I know enough of hate
To say that for destruction ice
Is also great
And would suffice.

This 1920 poem actually seems to address the conditions within the current American secondary school system. The desire that most students innately bring to the classroom is slowly "frozen" out of them over the course of 12+ years in that mind-numbingly conformist institution reductively and inaccurately called "school." And will the world end? Perhaps, at least metaphorically, it ends every day in America—every time another student becomes so disillusioned with the hated options and presumptions presented in schools that they despair themselves into depression, dropping out, addiction, or more frightening of all—conformity at the expense of authenticity.

For great teachers, the idea of filling the minds of a student as if knowledge were finite and liquid is an anathema. We know our own wisdom arrived in sparks and wafts of smoke, not in tidy measured containers. And yet, we persevere in a system that has forgotten its true mission. Inspired teachers look for the "aha!"

in students' eyes, and yearn for the spark even within the sodden and often moldy environs of the traditional American classroom.

"Pedagogue," by the way, is another fascinating word: Middle English's *pedagoge* derives from the Latin *paedagogus*, and Greek's *paidagōgos*, meaning a slave who escorted children to school. Ineffective education is like this—teachers like slaves ploddingly leading students in boring lessons in order to indoctrinate their minds. The American school system has, in some cases, degraded to the point where this is too often the rule rather than the exception. As teaching to the test—whatever godforsaken test it might be—has increased with No Child Left Behind and other misguided governmental "incentives," student joy has decreased proportionally.

It would not be an overstatement to say that over the past 15 years, the trend I have most commonly seen among students is an alarming level of apathy. Right at the moment when teens are organically and physiologically brimming with life, they are tuning out and going dead. How can this be? Have you ever seen a candle in a steam room? Hey, even the noblest flame eventually concedes to humidity. What could be sadder?

What can parents do about it? After all, schools are schools and the system is the system. Who are we to speak up? What do we know about such important matters as education and the proper purposes and modalities for educating youth?

We moms could follow the status quo, and fling ourselves back a hundred years. How simple it all must have seemed for those Victorian angels in the kitchen—until you read "The Yellow Wallpaper," and recall the madness that followed women's subjugated empowerment and voices. Or we could revert fifty years and don *Mad Men* dresses while not worrying our pretty little heads about things as masculinized and important in our culture as the training of young minds.

Even twenty-five years ago, the backlash against the feminism of the 1960s was well under way, as Gloria Steinem was pushed aside as female vox exemplar in the mainstream culture for edgier fare like messages from Madonna and Janet Jackson. Women swooned at the idea that "No one puts baby in a corner," forgetting that—probably due to Patrick Swayze's swoonability—Jennifer Grey was a woman in her mid-20s when *Dirty Dancing* was made. Far from a "baby," but oh how romantic it all seems even as the patriarchal systems strangling Grey's character demand she find a way to unleash herself.

Never mind all that. Women just keep falling in love and having families, and the world as it was, is, and has been—including the world of the American secondary school system—keeps going round in pretty much the same way. In some imaginary future version of *Dirty Dancing*, I imagine Baby driving a miniature version of herself to high school in a minivan, wondering how she got back into a corner consisting of entrusting this young colt of a woman to the suffocating ritual of school.

"The hand that rocks the cradle is the hand that rules the world," so the saying goes—and so it is. We moms have rocked the men whose procreative powers placed these students in our wombs and subsequent care. We have then rocked the cradles, rocked the PTA bake sales, and rocked our own career and homemaking paths. The one thing we have not yet, to date, rocked is the education system itself. The question begs asking: why not?

Why have the women of this country—who make up 80% of the teachers populating and 100% of the wombs necessitating this system—not fully awakened and mobilized ourselves for change?

Why have more of us not recognized that the broken-down inheritance of the outmoded, shallow, and stupefyingly damp American school system is harming our children?

Why have we not joined together, arm in arm, and combined our tremendous power as mothers, consumers, and voters to put an end to the tyranny of suppressive educational standards?

I have yet to meet a mother who is naïve enough to believe that she created her child. The *tabula rasa* is an idea that only a man could have initiated, and indeed it was Aristotle who wrote of the blank tablet in what is probably the first textbook of psychology, his treatise *De Anima* or *On the Soul*. After Aristotle the notion of the mind as an empty slate went largely unnoticed for more than 1,000 years. Yet the current educational system and many of the reforms discussed here seem to treat children as interchangeable buckets needing simultaneous and identical filling. The onus of individuated questions needing to be asked is removed. The oxygen of inquiry is replaced with dictatorial demagoguery.

We, who have populated the birthing chambers and bedrooms where these children were born—we know these are children, although they are seen by the dissociative institutions known as "schools" as mere students (or worse, potential score earners in a race to a non-existent top in a competition that exists only in the deluded minds of those who entirely miss the point of education). We recognize each as unique as the most proverbial snowflake and twice as fragile. Yet we allow a system as fundamentally flawed as the American education system gobble up those individual treasures in hopes that some day the child will grow to fruition as an adult and find their way to happiness in the world.

There is just one problem. Have you ever seen anyone happy without hope for finding their own true path? "Hope is a thing with feathers/That perches in the soul," wrote Emily Dickinson. Living in the shadow of a brutally patriarchal time and father, she sang the birdsong of hope. Her contemporaries in the Transcendentalist movement of the 19th century echoed the longing for hope for change from the rigidity of their era.

Another great thinker whom I've already quoted, Ralph Waldo Emerson, famously championed the notion that "character is higher than intellect" and that "imitation is suicide." He knew that authentic expression of each individual's perspective had more importance than intelligence. According to Emerson, people needed to tune out the overbearing commands of society in order to avoid becoming "the parrot of other men's thinking."

Moving back even further in time, Plato's "Allegory of the Cave" shows how wise the Greek philosophers were, and how far we have fallen from this level of awareness of the purpose of education. In Plato's narrative, Socrates describes a cave where people are chained from birth facing a wall. Behind them, puppets cast shadows on the wall in front of the prisoners. Who are the puppet-masters in today's system? Government agencies? School boards? Textbook publishers?

Because the chained people know nothing else, they assume the shadows constitute actual reality—but what they perceive is actually a misrepresentation of the real world. Socrates next reveals why institutions often resist philosophical education and how progressive education has to be to serve students. He does this by theorizing the result of unchaining the captives, and allowing them to turn toward the source of light that allowed those false perceptions to cast shadows in the first place.

At first, they'd be completely lost and confused, of course. When told that the experience in the cave was not entirely real, people would deny, resist even—and understandably so. It could almost be blinding to see the light of truth after a lifetime of illusion.

Just as I believe will happen with educational reform in the United States over these coming years, people's eyes must adjust slowly. First we might struggle to accept how far off the mark we've been for over a century, but eventually the sunlight of truth will bring into focus that which is needed—and no one will never want to return to the cave of puppetry and institutionalized indoctrination again.

I don't know about you, but I think our children have been chained in the cave of this broken American secondary educational system long enough.

Jesus Christ, arguably the greatest teacher the world has ever known, knew enough to:

- Teach by example, not just by words
- Openly rebel against the norms of his era
- Question authority
- Love his students by participating in their lives
- Ask questions as a way of leading students to discover their own answers
- Be willing to speak the truth even when the stakes were severe
- Weep when appropriate

No one wants to be crucified. In the Gospel story, Jesus' heart was broken when he heard his friend Lazarus had died. He wept not because he couldn't overcome death, because in fact he famously raised Lazarus a few verses later in the story. Perhaps he had to emotionally break, to engage his own heart strength, in order to power the enormous voltage that coursed through a dead man's veins and made him breathe again.

We can resuscitate the American education system. But first we need to soften our hearts and assess how dead our children have become.

When was the last time we wept? Look into the vacancy of their eyes. See the dearth of joy, and concession to obedience. What have we wrought? At what price have we allowed our children to be fodder in a gristly mill of governmental manipulations, corporate finagling, and institutionalized deceit?

Let's mourn our nation's educational shortcomings with wailing. And then, when our hearts have once again opened, and we remember who we once were, and who our children once were, and how this education system has failed us all—let us rise with the indignant power that only an army of loving mothers and fathers could generate, and shout in one loud voice: "Enough."

Addendum 3

A CALL TO ACTION

Children should be sent to schools to learn what they desire from life, not to memorize information in order to gather credits. The primary goal of education should be to generate definiteness of purpose within each student. The investment of time—12 years and often more—in schools should have a tangible and specific conversion into the spiritual, physical, emotional, and cognitive needs of life for all.

Students must be introduced to the working of their own minds. As Eckhart Tolle challenges: "Give up defining yourself— to yourself or to others. You won't die. You will come to life. And don't be concerned with how others define you. When they define you, they are limiting themselves, so it's their problem. Whenever you interact with people, don't be there primarily as a function or a role, but as the field of conscious Presence. You can only lose something that you have, but you cannot lose something that you are."

Educational reform advocate Sir Ken Robinson makes excellent sense in his numerous Ted Talks as he promotes ideas for change. A recent favorite of mine reminded us that our current system originated in the context of the Enlightenment and Industrial Revolution. Time has progressed, and so must we.

Ten Proposed Reforms: Academic

1. We must model for students permission to think for themselves, to fearlessly express their points of view, and to publically debate conflicting ideas with respect and a sense of both honor and humor.

2. Entire semesters should be devoted to teaching the use of mental focus to foster economic and practical freedom.

3. We must reconsider the philosophical view of the human brain as an organ that "thinks"—and prove to them the contrasting notion that it merely interprets stimuli, which simultaneously leads to what we call "thought." In breaking down the sequence, notions of "having to think or feel" a certain way about events or circumstances will be appropriately eradicated.

4. We must teach students the principles of success. This should emphasize the imperative to seek the seed of advantage sown in every "defeat," and the temporal nature of both concepts (success and failure).

5. Students must be granted the privilege to teach. By prioritizing firsthand realization and communication of knowledge, they will own what they learn.

6. Abstract concepts must be given their proper, and subordinate, status in favor of practical application of learning in a hands-on way. One example—the applicable skills needed for real life—e.g., how to balance a checkbook prior to prioritizing geometric theorems.

7. Original ideas must be celebrated, and conformity shunned. That said, students must learn to distinguish between knee-jerk rebellion and true originality.

8. Students must understand the concept of time as a finite asset that must be managed wisely, and create literal timelines of likely and possible milestones needed to build their own, unique, joyful futures.

9. We must resist our own resistance in underscoring the danger of believing anything on the mere basis of an authority figure—especially religious instructors, parents, and—yes—teachers.

10. We must teach the principle of reaping and sowing (Jesus), of karma (yogic sutras), and of the law of compensation (Ralph Waldo Emerson). Same principle, different names, crucial philosophical truth needing to be discussed in classrooms.

Ten Proposed Reforms: Personal

1. We must caution students against being hypnotized by the repetitive patterns of other people attempting to indoctrinate them. These habits of thought can become fixed and inhibit independent thought (and therefore definiteness of purpose outside the preferences of "society").

2. We must teach the psychological bases for all human behavior, and enable teens to apply these insights to making appropriate choices in all personal and business interactions accordingly.

3. We must insist that teenagers analyze the outcomes in life related to habit—both benevolent and malevolent—and have them examine real-life examples in their private

lives, as well as history and current events, that exemplify these relationships between the force of habit and the positive or negative result.

4. We must teach students to celebrate harmony within their own minds as the fruit of self-control.

5. We must teach the law of increasing returns, and the importance of going the extra mile.

6. We must illuminate the Golden Rule not as an abstract concept but as factual cause and effect—the way we treat others *is* the way we treat ourselves.

7. Without abstract condemnation, we must explain the supreme importance of the power of one's own will, and the destructive impact of cigarettes, alcohol, drugs, and over-indulgence in sex. Yes, I said sex. The lack of necessary discourse in this matter has become the root of serious confusion and subversion.

8. We must teach that the most effective way to bring about change in one's life is through a combination of definiteness of purpose and plans persistently pursued.

9. We must teach that the value of each human is measurable by the quantity and quality of service they render to others.

10. We must encourage teens with the fact that labels and words will forever fail to encapsulate the mysteries of life, and allow them to find meaning behind, beneath, and beside language.

With appreciation for Napoleon Hill, whose writings inspired these reforms.

IT'S TIME TO
OPEN THE GATE

You've got the Keys to College Admissions Success. Now it's time to use them to open the GATE.

Imagine the look on your child's face as they open the acceptance letter to the college of their dreams.

With the GATE System for College Admissions Success, that dream can become a reality. GATE is an acronym standing for the four mission-critical components of the training: Grades, Applications, Testing, and Essays.

GATE is a trademarked, exclusive system designed and developed by Pamela Donnelly and her team of elite educators. This unique curriculum provides unprecedented access to current trends, insights, and insider information, and is delivered in a way that connects with teens.

Secure their future. Open the GATE today.

Visit **www.gatesystemforcollegeadmissions.com.**

FOR PARENTS OF
COLLEGE-BOUND TEENS

The most successful people in business, athletics, and life all share one thing in common: a strong coach. Your teen deserves the same.

Pamela Donnelly's staff at Valley Prep Tutoring Services offers proven academic mentorship that will maximize your student's college acceptance success. These Ivy League tutors provide in-home, one-on-one support to secure top GPAs and test scores.

Mentorship provided in person where available, and worldwide via customized, friendly Skype sessions.

Apply today: **www.valleypreptutoring.com.**

Visit Pamela online:

www.PamelaDonnelly.com

CPSIA information can be obtained at www.ICGtesting.com
Printed in the USA
BVOW07*2339250115

384876BV00015B/177/P